Spinoza and Politics

to John Stachel,
a friend and comrade
for so many years!
Paris 16.12.98

Spinoza and Politics

ETIENNE BALIBAR

Translated by Peter Snowdon

VERSO
London • New York

First published by Verso 1998
This edition © Verso 1998
Translation © Peter Snowdon 1998
Preface © Warren Montag 1998
First published as *Spinoza et la politique*
© Presses Universitaires de France 1985
All rights reserved

This book is published with the financial assistance of the French Ministry of Culture

Verso
UK: 6 Meard Street, London W1V 3HR
USA: 180 Varick Street, New York NY 10014–4606

Verso is the imprint of New Left Books

ISBN 1–85984–801–X
ISBN 1–85984–102–3 (pbk)

British Library Cataloguing in Publication Data
A catalogue record for this book is available from the British Library

Library of Congress Cataloging-in-Publication Data
A catalog record for this book is available from the Library of Congress

Typeset by SetSystems Ltd, Saffron Walden, Essex
Printed by Biddles Ltd, Guildford and King's Lynn

CONTENTS

PREFACE *BY WARREN MONTAG*   vii

FOREWORD   xxi

NOTE ON EDITIONS AND TRANSLATIONS OF
    SPINOZA'S WORKS   xxiii

1 THE SPINOZA PARTY   1
   The "Freedom Party"   2
   Religion or Theology?   5
   Predestination and Free Will: The Conflict of Religious
       Ideologies   9
   Churches, Sects and Parties: The Crisis of the Dutch
       Republic   16

2 THE *TRACTATUS THEOLOGICO-POLITICUS*:
       A DEMOCRATIC MANIFESTO   25
   Freedom of Thought and the Right of the Sovereign   25
   Democracy: "The Most Natural" State   31
   A Philosophy of History?   36
   The Legacy of Theocracy   42

3 THE *TRACTATUS POLITICUS*: A SCIENCE OF THE STATE   50
   After 1672: A New Order of Problems   51
   The Plan of the *Tractatus Politicus*   56
   Right and Power   59

The "Body Politic"   64
Decision: The Soul of the State   71

4 THE *ETHICS*: A POLITICAL ANTHROPOLOGY   76
Sociability   76
What Is Obedience?   88
"Ethics" and Communication   95

5 POLITICS AND COMMUNICATION   99
Power and Freedom   101
"Desire Is Man's Very Essence"   105
The Aporia of the Community and the Question of
    Knowledge   113

CHRONOLOGY   125
FURTHER READING   129
INDEX   132

Preface

Warren Montag

Étienne Balibar begins his study of Spinoza's philosophy with the argument that it cannot be understood as if it existed only on the transhistorical, if not ahistorical, plane of pure theory and that, on the contrary, each of his major texts must be understood as an intervention in a specific political and philosophical conjuncture. For this reason, according to Balibar, it is impossible to separate Spinoza's metaphysics from his politics, as if the latter were an application of the former. Instead, Spinoza's philosophy must be seen as political in its entirety: even its most speculative utterances constitute responses to certain political imperatives and are tied to specific historical stakes. Thus, Balibar's title, *Spinoza and Politics* (as opposed to "Spinoza and Political Philosophy"), refuses at the outset the separation of philosophy into the speculative and the practical, a separation that is itself a perfect expression of the dualisms of mind and body and of the universal and the particular that Spinoza so vehemently rejected: all philosophy is political, inescapably embodied, no matter how it may strain to deny this fact, in the practical forms of its historical existence. Such an approach to philosophy demands much (perhaps too much, it will be said) of the reader: not only must we reconstruct the internal order of arguments that confer upon a given text its coherence and thus its self-sufficiency, but we must simultaneously understand the way a text belongs to and depends on a history outside itself whose play of forces, indifferent to the charms of reason, may precisely undermine the very coherence we thought we had discovered, surging up, as Balibar has put it elsewhere, to discompose or "incomplete" a given text.[1] Such notions will not surprise those

[1] Etienne Balibar, "The Infinite Contradiction", *Yale French Studies*, no. 88, 1995.

familiar with Balibar's intellectual itinerary, which is undeniably marked by a concern for the act of reading philosophical texts.

Of course, it is not only Spinoza's work that we must read as simultaneously conjunctural and "eternal" ("from the point of view of eternity", as Spinoza put it), but Balibar's as well. For given the close attention to the letter of Spinoza's Latin texts (and the reader will note how frequently Balibar's translator, Peter Snowdon, has been compelled to retranslate the citations from Spinoza, not because the existing translations are inadequate but because Balibar's argument is so closely tuned to the subtleties of Spinoza's Latin) and to the baroque complexities of power and politics in late-seventeenth-century Holland, it is easy to forget Balibar's text possesses its own conjunctural reality. It cannot be understood simply as a commentary on Spinoza but is also an intervention in the historical field to which it belongs.

At this point, readers are likely to recall Balibar's early career as a student and later a colleague of Louis Althusser, during which Balibar produced a significant body of work on Marx and Marxism. When the collective work *Reading Capital* appeared in 1965, its audience puzzled over the repeated references to Spinoza, a philosopher whose concerns seemed suspiciously distant from, if not antithetical to, those of Marxism. It was widely suspected that behind the texts of this period lay a fully developed interpretation of Spinoza, even a full-blown Spinozism that was offered to unwitting readers in the guise of Marxism. Perry Anderson spoke for many when he argued in *Considerations on Western Marxism* that "the systematic induction of Spinoza into historical materialism by Althusser and his pupils was intellectually the most ambitious attempt to construct a prior philosophical descent for Marx and to develop abruptly new theoretical directions for contemporary Marxism from it."[2]

Anderson did admit, if only in a footnote, that Althusser and company were not the first to assign Spinoza a privileged role in the "prehistory of dialectical materialism", to use August Thalheimer's phrase. Following Lucio Colletti,[3] however, he relegated

---

[2] Perry Anderson, *Considerations on Western Marxism* (London: New Left Books, 1976), p. 65.
[3] Lucio Colletti, *From Rousseau to Lenin: Studies in Ideology and Society* (New York: Monthly Review Press, 1972).

interest in Spinoza to the theoreticians of the Second International
(notably the Russian Marxist Plekhanov, who claimed to have
discussed Spinoza with Engels, shortly before the latter's death),
who presumably derived from Spinoza the "implacable determinism" that inspired their revision of Marx's thought.[4] In fact, as
Spinoza scholar (and former pupil of Althusser) André Tosel has
argued recently, the history of Marxist "detours" through Spinoza
(to use Althusser's metaphor) is far richer and more complex than
Anderson's note suggests;[5] a definitive account of this history
remains to be written. In each succeeding period of crisis within
Marxism, usually occasioned by a stabilisation and expansion of
capitalism after an economic and/or political crisis that was hailed
as "final", in the 1890s, the 1920s, the 1970s and 1980s, prominent
Marxists, many of whom (from Thalheimer to Negri) do not fit
the profile of the Western Marxist painted by Anderson, turned to
Spinoza's philosophy.

Why, of all the seventeenth-century philosophers, some of
whom, such as Hobbes and Gassendi, appear far more "materialist"
than Spinoza (whose Ethics, after all, begins with a discussion of
God), have Marxists been drawn to Spinoza? Beginning with
Feuerbach, whose theory of alienation is far more Spinozist than
has heretofore been acknowledged, there was a recognition that
Spinoza's treatment of "God, or Nature" was far more thoroughgoing in its elimination of every form of transcendence and ideality
than the work of many self-described materialists. In declaring God
to be the immanent cause of the world, Spinoza rejected not only
every dualism of spirit and matter, but also the dualisms of unity
and diversity, of the temporal and the eternal. In short, Engels
seemed to be speaking as a Spinozist rather than as a Marxist when
he defined materialism as the effort to "conceive nature just as it is,
without any foreign admixture",[6] that is, nature as an infinity of
singular existences. And while, until recently, Marxist readings of
Spinoza tended to focus on the Ethics at the expense of the Tractatus
Theologico-Politicus (TTP) and the Tractatus Politicus (TP), the materialism of Spinoza's approach to nature extends to his examination of

---

[4] Anderson, p. 65.

[5] André Tosel, Du matérialisme de Spinoza (Paris: Editions Kimé, 1994).

[6] Friedrich Engels, Ludwig Feuerbach and the End of Classical German Philosophy (Moscow:
Progress Publishers, 1969), p. 67.

social life: indeed, it could not be otherwise given Spinoza's insistence that the human world is not a "kingdom within a kingdom", part of nature but somehow not subject to its determinations. From this refusal of transcendence comes Spinoza's argument that political right can only have meaning when it is co-extensive with power in the physical, actual sense. Society then ceases to be characterised by a given set of rights or laws and becomes instead a relation of conflicting forces. Further, when right ceases to be formal, the central political relation can no longer be that between the individual as possessor of right and the state; when right is co-extensive with power, the individual who alone exercises little power is supplanted by what Spinoza in his last work calls, following Tacitus, Sallust and Machiavelli, the multitude or, as the term is rendered here, the masses. Thus, at a time when the conceptual foundations of liberalism were in the process of being established, Spinoza had already denounced the "constitutional illusions" (to borrow Lenin's phrase) of formal democracy in which powerless individuals "possessed" rights that "thousands of obstacles" prevented them from ever exercising.[7]

But if Balibar and his colleagues were once suspected of advancing Spinozism in the guise of Marxism, today it will rather be the opposite that is suspected of *Spinoza and Politics*: Balibar, with his emphasis on the centrality of "the fear of the masses" in Spinoza's philosophy (which signals a recognition that the masses and their movements constitute the primary object of political analysis), will undoubtedly be viewed by critics and admirers alike as "advancing Marxism by other means" in the 1980s, a time marked by its own fear of the masses and a consequent return to classical liberalism in both politics and economics. Indeed, in 1985 Balibar published an essay in the independent Left journal *Les Temps Modernes* entitled "Spinoza, the Anti-Orwell: The Fear of the Masses" in which he cites the untimely (*intempestif*) nature of Spinoza's politics in a time that sees "in mass movements only the figure of a radical historical evil".[8] In the anglophone world especially, where the few to have taken an interest in Spinoza's

---

[7] V. I. Lenin, *The Proletarian Revolution and the Renegade Kautsky* (Peking: Foreign Languages Press, 1970), p. 26.

[8] Etienne Balibar, "Spinoza l'anti Orwell", *Les Temps Modernes*, no. 41, September 1985, p. 37.

political writing tend to see him as a classical liberal in whose work one may discover the tenets of methodological individualism and rational choice theory, Balibar's arguments may well be taken as an attempt to put Leninist words in the mouth of one of Adam Smith's most illustrious forebears.

Both interpretations – Spinoza in the guise of Marx or the inverse – if inevitable, may now be said nonetheless to be wrong. It is true that Balibar, together with Althusser and others such as Pierre Macherey, during their period of collective activity viewed Spinoza as a privileged reference point in their project of reading Marx. It is not difficult to see the allure of Spinoza, who, as conceived by this group, was perhaps the most thoroughgoing materialist in the history of philosophy (even if his materialism, as Balibar remarks, was profoundly heterodox). In addition, Spinoza was one of the few philosophers to acknowledge the political stakes not only of the content of his work, that is, the arguments of which it is composed, but perhaps even more importantly of the form in which these arguments are realised, a form which will determine whether the philosopher's words will fall on deaf ears or whether they will allow readers to both recognise and seize the opportunity for improvement. As Spinoza remarked of Scripture, a text is to be judged sacred or profane, good or evil, not by virtue of what it says, or even its truth, but by its power to move people to mutual love and support. A philosophical work is thus always an intervention in a concrete situation and is to be judged by the effects it produces in this situation. This much can be gleaned from the works published by these philosophers in the sixties, from their scattered but provocative references to Spinoza. While they certainly read Spinoza with Althusser's encouragement, if not his guidance, they nevertheless did not produce any sustained work on Spinoza, certainly nothing resembling their "readings" of other philosophers. Indeed, despite rumours to the contrary, it appears that Althusser himself wrote and even lectured very little on Spinoza (although it is worth remarking how many of the most important Spinoza scholars in France today were members of Althusser's circle). Althusser's assertion in *Elements of Self-Criticism* that he, Balibar and Macherey "were Spinozists", which Anderson took as confirmation of his worst suspicions concerning Althusser's reliance on pre-Marxist thought, was nothing more than a retrospective construction, the very condition of which was a renaissance in French Spinoza studies that took place at the end of the sixties.

For, of course, they were not the only philosophers of note in France to have "discovered" Spinoza in the sixties. Another Marxist, although of an orientation different from and even opposed to Althusser's, laboured on what would become one of the monuments of contemporary Spinoza scholarship. Alexandre Matheron's *Individu et communauté chez Spinoza* (1969) argued that Spinoza's project was one of "disalienation", whose ultimate goal was a "communism of minds", defined as the whole of humanity becoming "a totality conscious of itself".[9] At the same time, Matheron's close reading of Spinoza's political texts (long neglected in favour of his so-called "metaphysical" writings, especially the *Ethics*) and his insistence on the importance of the multitude and of mass movements for Spinoza certainly influenced the young philosophers around Althusser. In fact, at Althusser's invitation, Matheron was a frequent guest lecturer at the Ecole Normale Supérieure (where Althusser was for many years head of the philosophy programme), together with another philosopher whose highly original reading of Spinoza attracted Althusser's interest: Gilles Deleuze. Deleuze's *Spinoza et le problème de l'expression* (1968), by focusing on the relatively marginal notion of expression in Spinoza, taught an entire generation of scholars to read Spinoza against the grain. In the interstices of the geometrical order of the *Ethics*, that is, in the prefaces, appendices and scholia to the propositions, could be found a second ethics, not so much offsetting the first as distilling its most important themes. Probably the most important work of the period, however, was the first volume of Martial Gueroult's *Spinoza* (*Dieu: Ethique I*) (1968), a nearly eight-hundred-page commentary on part I of the *Ethics*. Gueroult's approach shared with other "readings" (of Marx and Freud, for example) of the time a scrupulous attention to the letter of Spinoza's text, attempting to account for the totality of what Spinoza said (in part I) and to do so exhaustively, in a way that would in an important sense render all future commentary superfluous. This procedure, far from producing a dry (and prolix) copy of Spinoza's text, yielded some very surprising results. Gueroult

---

[9] Alexandre Matheron, *Individu et communauté chez Spinoza* (Paris: Minuit, 1969), p. 612.

showed that the most common interpretations of Spinoza's conception of substance and its constituent attributes and modes did not
correspond to Spinoza's philosophy as it was actually stated. In the
most fundamental sense, it appeared that no one before had really
read Spinoza to the letter.

Even as these three works recast the study of Spinoza, however,
they shared a concern to demonstrate the architectonic unity of his
major works. Paradoxically, the very care with which they adhered
to the letter of Spinoza's texts opened the way to a new set of
readings, equal in importance to the first, which began by acknowl-
edging that certain undeniable contradictions, conflicts and tensions, overlooked or explained away by the philosophers named
above, traversed his texts. The first of these, Pierre Macherey's
Hegel ou Spinoza, appeared in 1979. Macherey took Hegel's reading
of Spinoza, as presented in *The History of Philosophy* and *The Science
of Logic*, as one of the most rigorous and coherent interpretations of
Spinoza ever presented and an interpretation based solidly on
textual evidence. Hegel's critique of Spinoza centred on the
absence from the *Ethics* of two key concepts. First, substance as
subjectivity: Spinoza did not recognise the *Bildung* of substance
striving to become itself through the interiorisation of itself as
other. Second, substance could only become subject through the
operation of the second absent concept: "the labour of the
negative" that alone would permit substance to become itself
through the negation of its own negation. Macherey argues that
the absences Hegel claimed to see were in fact his own blind spots
(and perhaps even Spinoza's as well): Spinoza had already formulated a critique of the very positions that Hegel rightly regarded as
necessary to his own dialectic, even if it was left to Spinoza's
readers to elaborate it fully.

Did this mean that Spinoza's proleptic rejection of substance as
subject and the labour of the negative invalidated any notion of
history as dialectic? Macherey's spirited answer to this question was
a resounding no:

> It is Spinoza who refutes the Hegelian dialectic. But does this mean
> that in doing so he refutes every dialectic? Might it not just as well be
> said that what he refutes in the Hegelian dialectic is precisely what is
> not dialectical, what Marx himself called its idealism? For it is necessary

to set aside the idea according to which every dialectic would be in itself idealist or reactive as absolutely without philosophical interest: for a material history of thought, the expression "every dialectic" is completely devoid of meaning.[10]

From the confrontation between Hegel and Spinoza emerges the possibility of a dialectic without the negation of the negation and thus without the overcoming of contradiction, without finality of any kind, a dialectic of the positive.

Two years later the conversation continued with the publication of Antonio Negri's *L'anomalia selvaggia*, which was translated into French the following year, equipped with prefaces by Deleuze, Macherey and Matheron. This "extraordinary Marxist analysis", as Matheron called it,[11] marked the first recent attempt to move beyond textual analysis to a consideration of the historical and material circumstances of Spinoza's philosophical writing. Negri argued that the Spinozist anomaly was linked to the anomalous role of Holland in the world economy, specifically to its prematurity as a society that had consciously abandoned itself to the utopian lure of the capitalist market. The early Spinoza, argued Negri, exhibited a tension between a Neo-Platonism that was the philosophical expression of market ideology and an incipient materialism. His Neo-Platonism emphasised the priority of unity over diversity, the one over the many, the same over the different. Further, unity, the one and the same were all the outcome of a mediation that overcame diversity and difference. Such an idealism persisted even into the first two parts of the *Ethics*, constituting what Negri called Spinoza's first philosophical foundation. The *Tractatus Theologico-Politicus*, in turn, exhibited a tension between a juridical ideology of the social contract and a recognition of the power (and simultaneously the right) of the multitude. These philosophical tensions finally found their resolution in the materialism of the mature Spinoza (parts III–V of the *Ethics*, together with the unfinished *Tractatus Politicus*), a materialism of surfaces and singularities without mediation or transcendence and a political theory of the constitutive power of the multitude.

It is this context that allows us to appreciate the power and

---

[10] Pierre Macherey, *Hegel ou Spinoza* (Paris: Maspero, 1979), p. 259.

[11] Antonio Negri, *L'anomalie sauvage: Puissance et pouvoir chez Spinoza* (Paris: Presses Universitaires de France, 1982), p. 19.

originality of Balibar's *Spinoza and Politics*. To a far greater extent
than any other previous work, Balibar's is marked by a refusal to
dissociate the internal world of the texts from history conceived as
an exterior, as if they constituted in their ensemble a "kingdom
within a kingdom". Instead, he posits a continuity between writing
and history, treating the first as a prolongation of the second. To
separate nature/history (for nature, far from being an eternally
recurrent constant, is fully historical, just as history, that is, human
history, is part of nature considered as a process without a subject
or goals) from the world of ideas, even if only to establish
correspondences between them, would be to reinstate precisely the
dualism that Spinoza criticises at such length. Balibar is compelled
to establish in far greater detail than earlier commentators the
conflicts and contradictions of the Dutch Republic in the latter
half of the seventeenth century, for these are the very contradictions that form and inform Spinoza's philosophical project, even at
its most "metaphysical".

Balibar describes a society apparently divided into two camps:
on the one side, the urban and maritime bourgeoisie, who
accumulated tremendous wealth during the Netherlands' "Golden
Age" of commercial expansion and who were united around a
political doctrine of republicanism and a peculiarly tolerant form of
Calvinism that embraced religious pluralism and scientific progress;
on the other, primarily rural landowners, grouped around the
House of Orange, the Netherlands' would-be royal family, supported by the majority of Calvinists who hoped to end republican
government and install a monarchical-theocratic system. While it
is true that Spinoza supported the former bloc against the "Orangists" (and was friend and tutor to many members of the most
prominent Republican families), neither his philosophical project
nor, indeed, Dutch society itself can be reduced to this apparently
simple opposition between democracy and absolutism, and between
superstition and enlightenment. If we follow Balibar's reading of the
first and only exposition of Spinoza's theological and political views
published during his lifetime, the *Tractatus Theologico-Politicus*, we
may see it as both a critique of and a warning to his putative allies.

Certainly most of the work (fifteen of its twenty chapters) was
devoted to diminishing the power of superstition and thereby the
ability of the clerical enemies of the Republic to exploit religion in

their attempts to mobilise the people against the Regents. Spinoza systematically undermines every possibility that God's will (which he defines as the regular workings of nature) can be deciphered in unusual natural occurrences (miracles) or by a "deeper" interpretation of Scripture. Those who claim to be divinely inspired or who claim to see or know the real meaning of nature (its destiny) or Scripture have simply taken and attempted to persuade others to take their own imagination for reality. But the attack on any possibility of an appeal to the supernatural, as Balibar argues, had one extraordinary characteristic: it was carried out in the name of religion, that realm of the imagination that impels all people to look for hidden meanings and ultimate ends in the occurrences of nature (which, for Spinoza, includes society) and which is thus to some extent inescapable. The most powerful and effective arguments against religion must therefore be formulated in religious terms, systematically translating the language of theology into a language of reason or at least struggling to make such translation possible. Much, although by no means all, of his argument expressed views shared by a significant number of Republican supporters.

The political chapters of the *TTP* are a different matter altogether. When Spinoza announces that right is co-extensive with power and that big fish eat little fish by sovereign right, there can be little doubt that he is speaking not about individual subjects or citizens but about the "rightful" rulers of the Dutch Republic. For they appear to believe that their legality, their "legitimacy", offers some guarantee or protection against their enemies, even as their enemies have mobilised a substantial majority of the population against them, rendering the Regents' exercise of some of their rights impossible. Hence Spinoza's axiom that right equals power not only serves as a warning to Holland's Republican rulers that their right to rule is diminishing daily in proportion to the increase in the physical power of their enemies, but also reminds them that the only effective defence of their regime is a counter mobilisation rather than increasingly impotent appeals to legality. Such a warning, however, only revealed the undemocratic nature of Dutch democracy. The Republicans in fact constituted an oligarchy whose wealth gave them, for a time at least, the power to rule but which increasingly served to alienate popular support, especially as the defence of their extensive overseas commercial interests from

English and French interlopers necessitated a series of wars opposed by the rural elites and the urban masses. And there has been no state, Spinoza recalls at the beginning of chapter XVII of the *TTP*, that has not had more to fear from its own people than from any external enemy. Caught between a Republican party of progress whose democratic features were more formal than real and whose policies were dictated by the needs of a fabulously wealthy minority, on the one hand, and a party of monarchical reaction and religious fundamentalism with the active support of the masses, on the other, Spinoza in fact, as Balibar shows, expressed the perspective of a "freedom party still to be created".

In 1672, two years after the publication of the *TTP*, the Republic fell under the blows of a mass movement whose strength and ferocity startled contemporary observers. The *Tractatus Politicus*, arguably Spinoza's response to and analysis of the fall of Dutch republicanism, remained unfinished. There was no urgency attached to its appearance: it was not a work designed for the consumption of the literate reading public at large, as was the *TTP*. There is little or no mention of religion in the *TP*; it is strictly a treatise on politics. It is no accident, as Balibar maintains, that the work ends with a fragment of a chapter on democracy – all the more so given Spinoza's attempt to move beyond the conception of democracy as a formal system and to grasp it as an actuality subject to the ebbs and flow of mass movements, whose desires and actions cannot be predicted in advance. It is in the *TP* that Spinoza takes his postulates concerning power in the *TTP* to their logical conclusions. If right equals power, then the individual cannot be the unit of analysis: individuals alone have little power. Instead, at the centre of Spinoza's political analysis is the multitude, whose support, acquiescence or opposition determines the right of the (individual or collective) sovereign. In opposition to readers like Lewis Feuer who see in Spinoza a pure fear of the masses, Balibar argues that if a mass movement overthrew the Republic, a fear of the masses and their power equally prevented the solidification of a monarchic-theocratic system in post-Republican Holland. The multitude, which will not permit a violent or irrational ruler to rule very long, therefore must be considered at least potentially as the collective bearer of reason against the destructive passions of a single individual or small group of individuals. But what is the function of reason in human life and in human society? And since few follow the guidance of reason generally and no one follows it always, how do we increase its power? These are some of the questions that Spinoza takes up in the *Ethics*.

To begin to examine Spinoza's treatment of these problems we must first understand what sets him apart from nearly all of his contemporaries, who from Descartes to Hobbes and Locke regarded the isolated individual as the starting point of knowledge and society. For Spinoza there is no pre-social state of nature from which previously isolated individuals could emerge only through the juridical mediation of a contract. The atomic individual is the purest of fictions given that individuality or, better, singularity, a term that prevents us from taking the individual, indeed all individuals, as copies of a single model (self-interested, altruistic, depraved), is an effect of social existence. Just as we need a great many things external to us for the survival of the body (oxygen, water, nutrients) so our singular character (our *ingenium*) is formed by the rational and affective currents that flow through the collective. Neither reason nor the affects (or emotions) can be said in any rigorous sense to originate in the individual. Instead, Spinoza describes the process of the "imitation of the affects", the involuntary process of identification (which, although a mental phenomenon, is inseparable from our necessary corporal interactions with others), with its mechanisms of introjection, projection and projective identification: hatred and love, fear and hope, happiness and sadness circulate without origin or end.

What is the place of reason in all of this? As Balibar argues, reason, for Spinoza, in no way transcends the affects, which it would then have to master in order to be effective. Instead, Spinoza displaces the traditional opposition between reason and the emotions or affects with the opposition between passive and active affects. The latter increases the power of the body to act and simultaneously the power of the mind to think (the two powers for Spinoza are inseparable: there is no liberation of the mind without a liberation of the body), that is, in Spinoza's words, our ability to affect and to be affected by other bodies. Passive affects or emotions, in contrast, diminish our power to think and to act. Reason in a sense is thus immanent in active affects, in a kind of will to power that far from pitting us against individuals, as if power were a possession to be fought over, leads us to unite with them to increase our power: "there is nothing more useful to man than man" (*Ethics*, IV). Is it possible then that a certain corporeal-affective organisation of society would, if not insure, at least promote rational community (that is, the tendential dominance of active over passive affects)? It is. Is there any guarantee that such an organisation of society will ever come about or that were it to come about that it would endure? None whatsoever.

To read Spinoza carefully, that is, to enter the world of his philosophy, is to find oneself in a bewildering landscape bereft of all familiar reference points. Those who choose to follow Balibar's path, however, will discover in that landscape our own present, but in a form so defamiliarised that we can imagine the possibility of moving beyond it.

FOREWORD

I do not pretend to have found the best policy, but I know that I have discovered that which is true ... for truth is its own proof, as it is that of falsehood also.

Spinoza

He was a man who did not like constraints of conscience, and a great enemy of dissimulation.

Bayle

Spinoza and politics: at first sight, even this simple formula is a glaring paradox! If politics belongs to the order of history, here is a philosopher whose whole system is presented as the elaboration of the idea that to know is to know God, and that "God is nature" itself. If politics belongs to the order of the passions, here is a philosopher who sets out to know (*intelligere*) the desires and the deeds of men "in the geometric style ... as if it were a question of lines, planes and bodies" (*Ethics*, preface to part III). If politics is inherently bound up with present events, here is a philosopher for whom wisdom and the sovereign good consist in conceiving all singular things "from the viewpoint of eternity" (*sub aeternitatis specie*) (*Ethics*, V). What can he have to tell us about politics, that is not pure speculation?

Yet Spinoza himself saw no contradiction in welding together intelligence and conviction, concept and praxis. On the contrary. He began his *Tractatus Politicus* (*TP*) with these very notions, proposing to arrive at those conclusions "which accord best with practice", and to "deduce [them] from the real nature of man ... with the same objectivity as we generally show in mathematical inquiries". In this way, he hoped to come to know (*intelligere*) human actions by their necessary causes, and not merely "to deride, deplore, or denounce them" (*TP*, I, 4). The first of the major works of his maturity was the *Tractatus Theologico-Politicus*, a polemical work, a philosophical and political manifesto, which is marked throughout by both irony and anxiety, rising at moments to outright condemnation. Indeed, several close readers of these texts have been brought to the conclusion that Spinoza was unable to stick to his intentions, or that the primacy of the concept which he asserted was in fact only a mask for certain, all too human, passions.

In this short text, I wish to undertake an experiment. I propose to initiate the reader into Spinoza's philosophy *through* his politics. I intend thus to establish the unity of these two domains in Spinoza's thought, by a close reading of key passages from the three texts mentioned above.

Note on Editions and Translations of Spinoza's Works

There are two complete editions of the original texts (Latin or Dutch) of Spinoza's works: Van Vloten and Land, *Benedicti de Spinoza Opera Quotquot Reperta Sunt* (The Hague, 1895, 4 volumes; republished in 2 volumes), which does not contain the *Synopsis of Hebrew Grammar*; and Carl Gebhardt, *Spinoza Opera* (Heidelberg, 1924, 4 volumes), which corrects certain errors to be found in Van Vloten and Land, and is now the standard edition. Since its publication, several new letters have been discovered.

The English translation of Spinoza's works by Elwes (Dover) is far from entirely reliable and will be superseded by the new Princeton edition, edited and translated by Edwin Curley, of which only the first volume (of two), containing the *Ethics*, has so far appeared. In the present text I have therefore cited Spinoza's works after the following, admittedly somewhat disparate, translations:

Tractatus Theologico-Politicus, Samuel Shirley, trans., with an introduction by Brad S. Gregory (Leiden: EJ Brill, 1989);

The Letters, Samuel Shirley, trans., introduction and notes by Steven Barbone, Lee Rice and Jacob Adler (Indianapolis, Ind. and Cambridge: Hackett Publishing Company, 1995);

Tractatus Politicus, in *The Political Works*, A. G. Wernham, ed. and trans. (Oxford: Clarendon Press, 1958);

Metaphysical Thoughts (Cogitata Metaphysica), in *Opera*, C. Gebhardt, ed. (Heidelberg, 1924). This is the Latin text; the English translation is available in *The Collected Works of Spinoza*, Edwin Curley, ed. and trans. (Princeton, N.J.: Princeton University Press, 1985), vol. I;

The Ethics and *The Treatise on the Emendation of the Intellect*, in *The Collected Works of Spinoza*, Edwin Curley, ed. and trans. (Princeton, N.J.: Princeton University Press, 1985). This translation of the *Ethics* is also available in *A Spinoza Reader. The Ethics and Other Works* (Princeton, N.J.: Princeton University Press 1994) and is due to be published in the UK as a Penguin paperback;

The Ethics and Selected Letters, Samuel Shirley, trans., edited with an introduction by Seymour Feldman (Indianapolis, Ind. and Cambridge: Hackett Publishing Company, 1982).

I have throughout emended the existing English translations in the interests of terminological coherence, and to bring them into line with the French translations used or made by Etienne Balibar, where this seemed necessary in order to preserve the sense of both Spinoza's Latin and Balibar's argument. These alterations range from the restoration of historical nuances (soul, not mind, for *mens*; heart, throughout, for *animus*; City, not state, for *civitas*) to an insistence on preserving the visibility of cognate terms. At some points, where variations in translation were necessary to preserve some semblance of the English language, I have indicated in brackets the Latin word that might otherwise have been concealed (thus, for instance, the key term *utile*). See also the notes below on Spinoza's use of the term *imperium* and *affectus*.

References to the *Tractatus Theologico-Politicus* are given by the abbreviation *TTP* and the page number in the Shirley translation; to the *Tractatus Politicus* by *TP*, followed by the chapter and paragraph. References to *The Letters* cite the Shirley translation (1995). For the *Ethics*, I follow Curley's system:

Roman numeral = part
P = proposition
D = definition
C = corollary
S = Scholium
DefAff = definitions of the affects at the end of Part III.

—Trans.

1

THE SPINOZA PARTY

Brought out anonymously under the imprint of a non-existent publisher (but immediately attributed to the "atheist Jew of Voorburg"), the *Tractatus Theologico-Politicus (TTP)* caused a scandal that would not immediately fade away. It was, according to Bayle, "a pernicious and a hateful book". For over a century, a long catalogue of denunciations and refutations followed in its wake. But at the same time its arguments continued to leave their mark on fields as varied as biblical exegesis and "libertine" literature, political jurisprudence and the critique of traditional authorities.

Spinoza was far from unprepared for these violent reactions. In the preface, the extraordinary tension of whose prose can still be felt after all these years, he is fully aware of the double risk he runs. For his is a dangerously contradictory situation: he may be understood too well by those opponents whose instruments of intellectual domination he has set out to destroy, and yet not well enough by the great mass of his readers, even those whom he sees as his potential allies. Why take this risk then? In the preface he sets out to provide us with a detailed explanation: "I shall first set forth the causes that have induced me to write" (*TTP*, 52).

First among these causes is the degeneration of religion into a form of superstition, founded on the unreasonable fear of natural and human forces and on the self-serving dogmatism of the Churches. Superstition leads inevitably to civil war, whether overt or concealed (unless all dissent is stifled outright by despotism), and the manipulation of the passions of the many by those in positions of power. What can be done to remedy this? We can *distinguish between two types of knowledge* (a distinction which, as we shall see, is not an opposition): "knowledge by revelation", which can be

deduced from a rigorous reading of the Holy Scriptures and whose
object is "nothing other than obedience", and "natural knowledge"
– let us call it, provisionally, science or reason – which is concerned
only with Nature, in so far as it is accessible to universal human
understanding. "[T]hese two [kinds of knowledge] have nothing in
common, . . . they each have a separate province that does not
intrude on the other, and . . . neither should be regarded as
ancillary to the other" (*TTP*, 55). The first result of this distinction
will be the liberation of individual opinions in matters of faith,
provided that these opinions tend always towards the love of one's
neighbour; and this will be followed by a liberation of individual
opinions with regard to the State, provided that they remain
compatible with its security. In particular, there will be a total
liberation of philosophical research into God, nature and the paths
by which each man may attain wisdom and salvation. Whence
flows the definition of a *fundamental rule* for life in society: public
law will be "*such that only deeds may be arraigned, mere words never
being punishable*" (*TTP*, 50).[1] A State where this fundamental rule is
observed would be what Spinoza will later refer to as a democracy.
The "free Republic" of Amsterdam is one approximation of such
a State, though whether it is the best possible approximation, even
given the conditions prevailing at that time, remains an open
question. The Republic's existence, though, is under threat from
"absolutist" monarchists and theologians, in just the same way and
for just the same reasons as true Religion and philosophy are
threatened. Democracy, true faith (what the Scriptures call "charity
and justice") and philosophy are thus united in practice by a single
common interest. *That interest is freedom.*

The "Freedom Party"

Why then, if this is the case, does misunderstanding constantly
threaten, as if by anticipation, to undermine the arguments
advanced in the *TTP*? We can identify several reasons for this
predicament, which lie never far from the surface of the text.

In the first place, there is no notion more ambivalent than that
of "freedom". With very few exceptions, no philosophy, no

---

[1] This rule is derived directly from Tacitus, *Annals* I, 12. – TRANS.

political ideology (even those which are, in reality, forms of domination), has ever been presented as anything other than an exercise in liberation. That is why philosophical and political doctrine can rarely rest content with simple antitheses between freedom and constraint, or freedom and necessity. Instead, their arguments tend to take the form of an attempt to establish (or restore) the "true" definition of freedom in the face of opposition. Spinoza, as we shall see, provides us with an exemplary case of such a strategy.

But if this is so, it is not simply because the notion of freedom has always been beset by ambiguities and antinomies, independent of any historical context. The text of the *TTP* is shaped throughout by the circumstances in which it was written. It cannot be read as a work that exists only on one plane, that of "pure theory". The treatise is also Spinoza's intervention in a theological controversy that divided the society of his time. In it, he puts forward proposals that are intended to nip in the bud any collusion between the monarchist party and the "fundamentalist" propaganda of the Calvinist pastors. These aims were also those of the social groups with whom Spinoza was, of his own will, most closely associated during his lifetime; foremost among them, the governing elite of the Dutch Republic. For in fact this elite had by then begun to *describe itself as a "freedom party"*. It had grown out of a national liberation struggle. It championed civil liberties against a monarchist conception of the State similar to that which currently held sway over "absolutist" Europe. It defended freedom of individual conscience, the autonomy of scientific research and scholarship, and (up to a certain point) the free circulation of ideas. Yet was that enough to justify arrogating to itself exclusive rights to the term *freedom*? Spinoza, as we shall see, never took this self-proclamation at face value, even though he was a committed supporter of the "free Republic". In what the governing class presented as a self-evident solution, Spinoza saw a problem. How could freedom be identified with the politics of a particular group and its "universal" interest? Starting from this question, he came to define freedom in terms which were diametrically opposed to those used by his closest friends. That is, he elaborated an implicit critique of the illusion that sustained them in their conviction that they were fighting for a just cause. It is hardly surprising, then, that the *TTP*, which was written without any "revolutionary intention", seemed not only subversive to Spinoza's opponents, but more embarrassing than useful to his friends.

But the causes of this climate of misunderstanding can be traced back even closer to the heart of Spinoza's project. For if the *TTP* was written with a political aim, it is *in the medium of philosophy* that it seeks to construct its arguments. Two central questions run right through the book: one concerns the nature of certainty (and thus the relationship between "truth" and "authority"), the other the relationship between freedom and the right or "power" of the individual. Do philosophy and politics constitute *two* discrete domains? Is philosophy a "theory" from which a political "practice" might be deduced? And where did Spinoza obtain the philosophical idea of freedom with which he was able to unmask all illusions, even those of his friends and political allies? By the end of this work, I hope to make intelligible what there may not be space to demonstrate: that the relationship between philosophy and politics is such that *each implies the other*. By posing specifically philosophical problems, Spinoza is not choosing to approach his political concerns by an indirect route, he is not transposing them from their proper place and recasting them in a "metapolitical" medium. He deals in philosophical terms because only philosophy can give him the means to know exactly or, as he would say, "adequately" (cf. *Ethics*, IID4, IIP11, 34 and 38–40; and *The Letters*, LX) the power relations and the particular interests that are at stake in politics. For only thus can he know them *by their causes*.

At the same time, structuring his philosophical investigation around political questions will not distract him from his inquiry into the essence of philosophy. On the contrary, it is one way of determining the true interest and the true problems of philosophy. (Whether it is the only way, it is too early yet to say.) From this point of view, the dilemma which would have us distinguish between "speculative" philosophy, on the one hand, and philosophy "applied" to politics, on the other, is not simply meaningless, it is the *principal obstacle* to achieving wisdom. Yet the kind of unity this implies is far from straightforward and easy to understand. Spinoza himself only began to grasp its nature when he had reached the end of an intellectual experiment in which philosophy as a discipline was forced to question and rectify the prior certainties ("illusions"?) on which it rested. *The TTP is this experiment.* In concrete terms, this means that, as the text progresses, the conception of philosophy around which it is organised is not fixed but is constantly changing. Spinoza's thought is undergoing a transformation from within. This transformation is necessary, yet its consequences cannot wholly be foreseen. It is all the more difficult to define this process as it brings into question a relationship that involves not just two terms but three (philosophy, politics *and* theology), or even four (philosophy, politics, theology *and* religion). If we want to understand more clearly what is at issue here, we will have to begin by reconstructing the manner in which these different domains presented themselves to Spinoza.

Religion or Theology?

That the writing of the *TTP* represented a turning point for Spinoza is clear from his correspondence, in particular the correspondence with Oldenburg. Again and again we find evidence of the insistent demands that were made on Spinoza once he had begun to make public, in conversation or in writing, selected elements of his "system":

> Now I shall turn to matters that concern you and me, and here at the outset let me be permitted to ask whether you have completed that little work of such great importance, in which you treat of the origin of things and their dependence on a first cause, and also of the emendation of our intellect. Of a surety, my dear friend, I believe that nothing can be published more agreeable and more welcome to men who are truly learned and wise than a treatise of that kind. (*The Letters* XI, 1663, p. 99)

But Spinoza, though he continued to work on the *Ethics* and to correspond with his friends on scientific and metaphysical subjects, managed in practice to evade the demands that were being made upon him. Towards the end of 1665, in a letter to Oldenburg, having described the evolution in his philosophical thinking, he adds:

> I am now writing a treatise on my views regarding Scripture. The reasons that move me to do so are these: 1. The prejudices of theologians. For I know that these are the main obstacles which

prevent men from giving their minds to philosophy. So I apply myself to exposing such prejudices and removing them from the minds of sensible people. 2. The opinion of me held by the common people, who constantly accuse me of atheism. I am driven to avert this accusation, too, as far as I can. 3. The freedom to philosophise and to say what we think. This I want to vindicate completely, for here it is in every way suppressed by the excessive authority and egotism of the preachers . . . (*The Letters*, XXX, p. 186)

Note the reference to contemporary politics: the accusation of atheism, directed at a friend of the governors of the Republic, figured in the sermons of Calvinist pastors, who were manoeuvring to impose their version of religious orthodoxy. But the principal idea, which corresponds to the central argument constantly reiterated throughout the *TTP*, is the *radical separation of the domains of philosophy and theology*. Let us pause for a moment to examine this point. What exactly does it mean, in this context, to speak of "separation"?

The formula in itself is not entirely original. Descartes, for example, in his *Metaphysical Meditations* (1641, translated into Dutch by a friend of Spinoza), had proclaimed the separation of the two "certainties" of Reason and of Faith. Metaphysical demonstration was the exclusive province of the former. The question of revelation and of the traditional foundation of the Churches' authority was left entirely to one side.[2] All the signs were that the treatise on "first philosophy", which was to found the certainties of the new mathematical and experimental science of nature and which Oldenburg and others expected Spinoza to write, would proceed from such a perspective. The confrontation with theology would then arise as a *secondary*, external question, due to the censorship which that discipline sought to impose upon "natural philosophy" in the name of an out-dated dogma. Theology was important because through its intellectual influence and its official

---

[2] "Note that I do not consider at all . . . the question of sin, that is to say of the error that is committed in the pursuit of good and evil: but only that error which may occur in judging and discerning what is true and what is false. And I have no intention of speaking of those things that belong to faith, or to the conduct of life, but only of those which concern those speculative truths which can be known with the aid of natural light alone." Descartes, *Meditations, Synopsis*, in *The Philosophical Writings of Descartes*, trans. John Cottingham, Robert Stoothoff and Dugald Murdoch (Cambridge: Cambridge University Press, 1984), vol. II, p. 15; translation modified.

authority it could hinder the true metaphysics from gaining due recognition. For men to think and study in accordance with the truth, all they needed was to be free of this interference, and to "emend their intellect" in all the domains to which it could be correctly applied, by stating clearly the principles that were proper to it.

But what if the obstacle that was theology should "resist" and refuse to leave the field to its rival, even when the truth had been laid bare for all to see? Might it not be necessary to attack it directly, in and for itself? That is, might it not be necessary to elaborate a *double* critique of theological discourse in its two interrelated aspects, as *both* the ideology of a socially powerful caste *and* a general form of relationship to the objects of knowledge, a general form of "certainty"? Thus Spinoza found himself confronted by a new, and much more disturbing, question than that with which he had started. For his problem · now was, Where exactly does the boundary between philosophy and theology lie? If knowledge develops at the same time along two entirely independent paths, one followed by its applications and the other by its theoretical principles, and if it is by reason alone that it can determine and describe the "first cause" and the universal laws of nature – or "eternal verities" – then does it not inevitably follow that knowledge is grounded not only on a metaphysics but also on a theology, be it explicit or implicit? The philosopher-scientist who halts his advance once the traditional theological obstacle to knowledge has been removed may well find himself taken prisoner by another, more subtle, theology. Indeed, was that not what had happened to Descartes and was later to befall Newton?

The central paradox of the *TTP* will then come as less of a surprise to the reader who has followed the argument thus far: the principal object to which philosophy must be applied, once it has been freed from all theological preconditions, is the validity of the biblical tradition and the question of the true content of Faith. Taken to its extreme, philosophical rationalism thus seems to contradict its initial premises, for its purpose is now to remove the confusion that is hidden within the term *theology*. That is, its aim has become to *free faith itself from theology* and denounce theology as a philosophical "speculation" that is foreign to "true Religion".

[A]though religion as preached by the Apostles – who simply related the story of Christ – does not come within the scope of reason, yet its substance, which consists essentially in moral teachings as does the whole of Christ's doctrine (in effect, the teachings of Jesus in the Sermon on the Mount, related in Matthew, chapter 5), can be readily grasped by everyone by the natural light of reason. (*TTP*, 201–2 and n. 27)

Scriptural doctrine contains not abstruse speculations or philosophic reasoning, but very simple matters able to be understood by the most sluggish mind. I am therefore astonished at the ingenuity displayed by those ... who find in Scripture mysteries so profound as not to be open to explanation in any human language, and who have then imported into religion so many matters of a philosophic nature that the Church seems like an academy, and religion like a science, or rather, a subject for debate. ... Scripture's aim was not to impart scientific knowledge ... Scripture demands nothing from men but obedience, and condemns not ignorance, but only obstinacy. Furthermore, since obedience to God consists solely in loving one's neighbour ... it follows that Scripture commands no other kind of knowledge than that which is necessary for all men before they can obey God according to this commandment. ... (Other philosophic questions which do not directly tend to this end, whether they be concerned with knowledge of God or with knowledge of Nature, have nothing to do with Scripture, and should therefore be dissociated from revealed religion.... [T]his matter is of cardinal importance to the concept of religion ... (*TTP*, 214–15)

Spinoza thus found himself in an extremely awkward position. His critique of philosophy was now that it was not only anti-philosophical but anti-religious! Having set out to defend freedom of thought against theology, he had ended up writing an apologia for *true Religion* (still conceived of as a revealed Religion) which was also an attack upon philosophers! It now seemed that the single enemy facing both those who seek after truth and those who practise obedience was a certain dominant "metaphysical-theological" discourse. Spinoza was thus running the risk of taking on two adversaries at once, the theologians and the majority of philosophers: the former, because they made their living by speculating rationally on religious objects, thus transforming them into theoretical objects; and the latter, because they tended to distort philosophy into an anti-religious discourse.

However, Spinoza himself has to face several difficult questions.

Where exactly does the boundary lie between faith and those speculations through which it degenerates into "superstition"? Spinoza allows that certain philosophical theses or "truths" are necessary presuppositions if we are to understand how obedience, love and salvation are united, and that these "truths" are problematic. The use of a double terminology – *revealed* Religion/*true* Religion – is itself a symptom of this difficulty. On the other hand, how are we to explain the emergence of theological discourse? Is there a tendency already present within religion itself to pervert its own aims? Is there a need for theoretical speculation which is inherent in the mass of humankind (the "vulgar") and from which theologians then derive their authority? Is theology the straightforward manipulation of the masses by the clever and the devious? Or should we not see superstition as a form of *reciprocal dependence* between the faith of the "vulgar" and "learned" religion, in which the actors on both sides of the relationship are equally trapped?

Predestination and Free Will: The Conflict of Religious Ideologies

Spinoza's investigation into theology, that is, into the forms taken by the theological confusion between religion and speculative thought, is carried out on two levels: doctrinal and historical. His inquiry traces the situation back to its "origins" in order to grasp what is happening in the present. In doing so, he goes far beyond an external description of the discourse in question, to analyse its underlying logic. The results thus provide Spinoza with the material for what will become, in the *Ethics*, a general theory of the *imagination* (cf. especially the appendix to part I).

There is a Mosaic theology: founded on a cosmology of creation and miracle, an ethic of obedience and an eschatology of the "chosen people", it serves to justify the commandments of the Hebrew law and to explain them to the mass of people of that time and of that nation (*TTP*, 81–4, 107, 130, etc.). This does not mean that Moses constructed an artificial ideology in order to dominate his fellow citizens: on the contrary, he himself believed in the revealed truth of his theology, of which he had been granted incontrovertible "signs", and it was this faith that enabled him to found a State and a religion. Likewise, there is a theology, or more precisely, there are *several theologies belonging to the prophets*, which contradict each other on certain crucial points (*TTP*, 85–6, 145): in particular, they are already divided on the question of salvation (does it depend solely on divine election, or also – and if so, in what way – on our deeds, good or bad, in accord with the law, or not?). These differences in teaching exhibit one essential feature of theology: that it *introduces conflict* into religion. Differences of this kind are to be found in an even more exaggerated form in primitive Christianity (between the doctrines of the different Apostles, and in particular between Paul, James and John) (*TTP*, 108, 203). They will ultimately be institutionalised as the divisions separating the contemporary Churches.

The *question of grace* had long been a subject of theological controversy. If man is a sinner – guilty of an original crime that lives on in the attraction he feels to evil, in the fact that he "desires what is forbidden" – then he cannot be saved except through divine mercy. It is this mercy which is made manifest in history through the mediation of Christ, redeemer of humanity and incarnation of grace. But what is it to "live in Christ"? What is the "way" of salvation? How does the "efficacy" of grace operate? In these age-old questions, it is the whole issue of how we represent the personal relationship between mortal man and immortal God that is at stake. Such questions acquired a new urgency after the Reformation in the debates that ensued about faith, ascesis and the examination of conscience, and the roles of inner discipline and pastoral direction in the life of the good Christian. Calvin, who would never make any concessions to the powers of fallen humanity, presented his theology of salvation through grace alone as a return to the orthodoxy of Paul and Augustine. He denounced the idea of salvation through "works" as human pretence – whether these works were performed by observing the commandments, so as in some way to guarantee divine mercy, or through the "free" cooperation of man's will in his liberation from sin. In his eyes, both these idea were attempts by God's creatures to "glorify themselves" before their creator, and that desire was the essence of sin itself. He effectively polarised the debate to come, by setting the doctrine of *predestination* in opposition to the doctrines of free will. According to the doctrine of predestination, salvation has *always already* been decided by God, so that men are divided in advance into the "elect" and the "damned". Far from their actions having any influence on God's grace, it is grace which, mysteriously, gives and takes away the power to love Him exclusively. In the seventeenth century this controversy did not split the Christian community along denominational lines, setting Roman Catholicism against the Protestant Churches, but divided each of these two camps internally. In France, the Jesuits were opposed by the Jansenists, who sought to fight the Calvinists with their own weapons and were intransigent on the question of salvation by grace alone. In Holland, the two opposing factions were the orthodox pastors, who defended predestination, and the "Arminians", named after the theologian Harmensen (or Arminius), who supported the theory of free will.

In the *TTP*, Spinoza was, in his own way, taking part in this debate. But the propositions he put forward were such that they could not possibly satisfy either camp. According to Spinoza, the doctrine of Scripture, once separated from certain circumstantial variations, was constant and unequivocal:

> faith does not bring salvation through itself, but only by reason of obedience; or, as James says (ch. 2 v.17), *faith in itself without works is dead*. . . . [I]t follows that he who is truly obedient necessarily possesses a true and saving faith. . . . From these considerations it again follows that only by works can we judge anyone to be a believer or an unbeliever. (*TTP*, 222)

The fundamental dogma of true religion is, in fact, that love of God and love of one's neighbour are really one and the same. This might appear to lead to a theology of free will, or at least to a critique of predestination. But the salutary value of charitable action towards one's neighbour is not, on this theory, the result of a choice between good and evil, but of simple obedience. Moreover, Spinoza leaves no place for the idea of repentance, nor for that of "redemption" from original sin. In fact, original sin is entirely eliminated from his scheme; it is nothing more than an imaginary representation that accompanies a man's actions when they are detrimental to the man himself (an "unhappy conscience": the theory of religious sadness will be elaborated in the *Ethics*). It is as if Spinoza, having repudiated the last trace of fatalism that had persisted even among the theorists of free will, was now pushing their thesis to its extreme point – a point to which they, as Christians, were not prepared to go. For now, the entire question of the religious value of a man's works is reduced to the intrinsic quality of the present action.

The reader who is uncomfortable with this distortion of existing doctrine will be even more uncomfortable with the other strain in Spinoza's thought. For when he comes to discuss the "election" of Israel (which for Christians is the prototype of the individual's election through the grace of God), we find him writing that "since no one acts except by the predetermined order of Nature – that is, from God's eternal direction and decree – it follows that no one chooses a way of life for himself or accomplishes anything except by the special vocation of God, who has chosen one man before others for a particular work or a particular way of life" (*TTP*, 90). Is it not in this instance the thesis of predestination that Spinoza seems to support? Indeed, he delights in quoting Paul's formula (Rom. IX: 21) according to which man is in the power of God "like clay in the hands of the potter, who from the same lump makes one vessel to honour and another vessel to dishonour" (*TTP*, 307 n. 34; cf. *Metaphysical Thoughts*, vol. I, pp. 243ff.; *TP*, II, 22). From this standpoint, free will is a mere fiction. But again there is a crucial difference: Spinoza does not identify the "eternal will of God" *with grace*, in opposition to human nature; in a striking and decisive move, he identifies it *with nature* itself, in its totality and its necessity. This thesis is fully developed in chapter VI of the *TTP* (on miracles): if we can say that God has predetermined everything, then that is because God is here understood as "Nature's eternal laws" (*TTP*, 128). "So if there were to occur in Nature anything that did not follow from her laws, this would necessarily be opposed to the order which God maintains eternally in Nature through her universal laws. So this would be contrary to Nature and Nature's laws, and consequently such a belief would cast doubt on everything, and *would lead to atheism*" (*TTP*, 130). Any other idea of divine power would be absurd: it would be tantamount to imagining that God should contradict himself and infringe his own "laws" for the benefit of man. Thus Calvinist theology too, for all its rigorous "theocentrism", is the result of a compromise with humanism.

Both the "liberal" theologian and the theologian who believes

in predestination see redemption as a miracle: the one as a miracle
of the human will over natural necessity (or the flesh), the other as
a miracle of divine grace that must "overcome" the perverted
liberty of human beings. These competing theologies share a
common fiction: that of a *moral or spiritual world* opposed to the
natural world. Once this fiction has been eliminated, the question
of the relationship between human freedom and the order of the
world will no longer appear as an unsettling enigma but as a
practical problem, rationally intelligible if not easily soluble. Spinoza sets out to demonstrate this by turning the theses of the
theologians back on themselves, so that they undermine their own
original intentions. Once this has been achieved, he himself will be
able to propose a "definition" of salvation that includes temporal
happiness (security, prosperity), moral virtue and knowledge of the
eternal truths (*TTP*, 89–91, 104–5).

Why does he engage in a "dialectic" that is so corrosive and
dangerous? Why does he not just directly state that salvation is the
fruit of obedience to a rule for life that is both charitable and just,
and which is equally as binding for the "wise man" who is able to
conceive of natural necessity as it is for the "ignorant man" for
whom "it is better, indeed essential, to consider all things as
possible" (*TTP*, 102; translation modified)? (Intellectual inequality
between men does not make any practical difference.) If Spinoza
does not adopt a more direct method, it is because the idea of a
"rule for life" still contains within itself the notion of a law. In
translating the "eternal decree of God" as "the universal laws of
Nature", we have merely shifted the notion from one ground to
another. Until we are actually able to shed some light on the
meaning of this metaphor (which is the aim of chapter IV of the
TTP), we will never break out of the vicious circle of theology.
We cannot proceed with the question of the difference between
true Religion and superstition/speculation until we have removed
this obstacle.

The laws of Nature "are not adapted to religion (whose sole aim
is the good [*utile*] of man) but to the order of Nature as a whole,
that is, to God's eternal decree, which is beyond our knowledge.
This truth seems to have been glimpsed by those who maintain
that man can sin against the revealed will of God, but not against
the eternal decree by which he has pre-ordained all things" (*TTP*,

247; translation modified). What the Calvinist theologians had "glimpsed" was the disproportion between the *power of man* and that of *nature as a whole* on which he depends. Onto this disproportion, which caused them as much anxiety as it did other men, theologians of all kinds had projected a fundamental illusion: they "imagined God as a ruler, law-giver, king, merciful, just and so forth; whereas these are all merely attributes of human nature, and not at all applicable to the divine nature" (*TTP*, 107). They imagined "two powers quite distinct from each other, the power of God and the power of Nature", as if the power of God was "like the power [*imperium*] of some royal potentate, and that of Nature was like some blind force" (*TTP*, 124; translation modified). Thus the history of Nature appeared to them in the guise of a cosmic drama, in which the victory of Good over Evil was at stake and which was working itself out, using human actions as its instruments. Some of these theologians saw God as a judge who was capable of a certain flexibility, from whom men could obtain forgiveness by showing him proofs of their love, even if, in these conditions, their "freedom" of action was always dependent upon the will of the master who had put them to the test. Others, who were less optimistic, imagined him as a judge who was strict and unbending, who had decided once and for all, at random, which men would be faithful to him and which would rebel, thus denying them any real freedom, so as to keep it all for himself.

But whatever the case, whether we tend towards a "contractual" or an "absolutist" image of God's power and his law, the image we make is nothing more than an anthropomorphic transposition, attributing to God patterns of behaviour drawn from our experience of relationships between men. In so doing, these patterns are idealised, stripped of any human limitation or "finitude". By conceiving God's will as an example of "free will", a power to do or to refrain from doing, to give or to refuse, to create or to destroy, albeit on a scale which is "infinitely beyond" that of any human power, theologians and philosophers had created a fantastical picture of the "psychology of God". This picture would serve Spinoza as the prototype of the *imagination*, that inadequate knowledge of natural relationships which is the necessary consequence of man's relative impotence. This fiction derives from our common experience that it is impossible to live without desiring salvation (happiness, security, knowledge) and equally impossible to have immediate knowledge of real causality. Real causality is that which is immanent to the process through which all things are continuously being transformed. It excludes both "chance" and "design". By projecting human impotence onto nature as a whole, through the inverted figure of an anthropomorphic God, the theologians compounded our original confusion with an additional obscurity. They created a "refuge for ignorance" from which ignorance can only be extricated with difficulty. And in doing so, they not only rendered the idea of God totally incomprehensible, they went on to hold this obscurity as a dogma which itself expressed the essence of God.

There is nothing gratuitous about this paradox. In the first place, it brings with it benefits which are by no means secondary from the point of view of the theologians, for it casts them in the role of indispensable intermediary between God and man. They alone are able to interpret the divine will. Inevitably, what began as an indirect benefit becomes in time an end in itself, as the theologians seek to establish their power, even if it is only the power (which may seem slight, but is, in practice, exorbitant) to *teach* everyone what they must think and do at every moment if they are to obey God. That they are themselves the first victims of the illusions on which their ambitions are grounded only serves to add a fanatical dimension to their tyranny. After all, the most despotic master is the one who believes he has received a sacred mission to save those whom he dominates, and who sees himself as the humble servant of another Master, whose will cannot conceivably be resisted. In the second place, the element of anthropomorphism found in theological representations is not just an indeterminate fiction. It is an essentially *monarchical* figure, and an idealised one at that. Christianity, once it had constituted itself as a Church, only affirmed that "God was made Man" in the person of Christ in order to bolster the monarchical image of the Judge (in the "kingdom of God", Christ is seated on the right of his father's throne). And the Christian kings did not hesitate to use this ideological representation to guarantee the sacred origin of their temporal power. Every sacred figure of power is an expression of men's inability to see themselves as fully responsible for their own collective salvation (*TTP*, 253–4).

But might not this "theological need", in its given historical forms, be less the result of a general weakness in human nature than of a specific kind of social order? Might it not stem from the inability of human individuals to organise their relationships with each other in a fully conscious way? Thus the argument with which we began, concerning the relationship between religion, theology and philosophy, has now led us onto a territory which is, in fact, the territory of politics itself.

Churches, Sects and Parties: The Crisis of the Dutch Republic

The *TTP* was written over a period of several years. This was a time of crisis throughout classical Europe – of endemic revolts, revolutions, wars and epidemics – and in particular for the United Provinces. The country was crucial to the "balance of power" in Europe which was then beginning to take shape, and its rulers even hoped that one day they might come to exercise an undisputed hegemony over this system. This was the period which historians would later refer to as Holland's Golden Age.

Since the revolt of the Gueuzen in 1565, Holland had been almost continuously at war. The dynamics of mercantile expansion, based on the establishment of monopolies both of markets and of colonies, led automatically to a permanent state of war. Despite the strength of their navy, the Provinces had been invaded and overrun several times. Each time this occurred, it put the issue of establishing a real nation-state back on the political agenda. Through the war of independence, each of the Provinces had obtained a considerable degree of autonomy. Both in foreign and domestic affairs, the contest was between two opposing policies, which were supported by two rival groups within the ruling elite.

The house of Orange-Nassau, descended from the former counts of the country, traditionally held both command of the army and the executive function of "stadholder". Alongside them were a group of bourgeois "Regents", who were responsible for the administration of the cities and for managing public finances. At the provincial level, these tasks were entrusted to officers known as "pensionaries", while the finances of "Their Great Powers, the Estates-General of the United Provinces" were entrusted to a "Councillor Pensionary". The running conflict between these two groups had been marked by three major crises in the course of the seventeenth century. In 1619, the Councillor Pensionary Olden-barnevelt was accused of treason and of conspiring with the Arminian pastors, and was condemned to death at the instigation of the stadholder, Maurice of Nassau. The house of Orange was ambitious to obtain a hegemony over the State. But at the same time, the influence of the bourgeois companies (the East and West India Companies and the Bank of Amsterdam) was growing rapidly. Between 1650 and 1654, just after the Provinces had won their definitive independence, there was a new crisis, which overturned the balance of power: for the first time, the House of Orange tried to push the State towards a monarchy, but the attempt failed. The principal leader of the Regents' party, Johan de Witt, was made Councillor Pensionary of Holland and decreed, first, that the House of Orange be excluded in perpetuity from holding military office and, second, that the post of stadholder be abolished. From the 1660s onwards, the Orange party, under the leadership of the young William III, the future king of England, sought in turn to undermine the power of the Regents. This period of agitation culminated in a popular uprising in 1672, which coincided with the French invasion. Johan de Witt and his brother were hacked to pieces by the mob, and the post of stadholder restored with new, more extensive powers. In the end, the "stadholderless Republic" had lasted only twenty years.

Both the Regents and the Orangists had emerged from the elite that had conducted the war of national independence. To the extent that different groups rallied behind them, they can be described as representing the interests of different classes. But it is here that a major paradox emerges. The princes of Orange were, in the first instance, the leaders of a small landowning aristocracy in the "inner" provinces, while the Regents belonged to an extensive bourgeoisie made up of city dwellers, ship owners, industrialists and merchants. There always were and always would be many bonds, both of friendship and of interest, between the Orange aristocracy and the merchant bourgeoisie. But the Regents' group had seen its wealth grow to fabulous proportions over the course of half a century and had itself become a caste. The directors of both the financial companies and the collegiate public insti-tutions were appointed by co-option from among the members of a small group of closely interrelated families (the Witts, the Beuningens, the Burghs, the Huddes, and so on). They thus isolated themselves more and more from the bulk of the middle classes (artisans, merchants trading within the Provinces, fisher-men), who were increasingly deprived of any real share of power. Moreover, thanks to the progress of capitalist accumulation, the rural poor were soon joined by a deprived urban proletariat, concentrated in Amsterdam and Leiden, who lived in a permanent state of latent revolt.

However, social stratification in itself would never have led the "multitude" to identify with the Orange cause had there not been a convergence of two different crises – one military, the other religious – which posed the crucial question of the *relationship between Church and State*.

In the United Provinces, Calvinist reform combined the rejec-tion of "Roman idolatry" with anti-Spanish (and later anti-French) patriotic feeling. Calvinism became the official religion of the country but was never its only religion. A significant Catholic minority maintained the right to organise. Similar protection was granted to the prosperous Jewish community in Amsterdam, which was principally of Spanish and Portuguese extraction. But it was the division of Dutch Calvinism itself into two branches that was responsible for overdetermining the nature of social conflict and the identity of the political "parties" throughout this period.

The first branch was that of the *Remonstrants*, named after the proponents of the Arminian theology who had addressed a "Remonstrance" to the Estates-General in 1610 outlining their political and religious positions. They believed in free will and placed great importance on freedom of conscience, which led them to argue for religious tolerance. In this respect they were following the tradition of Erasmus. They wished to establish a "religious peace", which would reduce the power of the ecclesiast-ical corporations and leave responsibility for the individual's salva-tion to the individual in question. They were opposed to the discipline of obedience, which was constantly enjoined upon the faithful in the preaching of the Church. Instead, they made a distinction between *outward religion* (institutional forms), to which they assigned a merely pedagogical function, and *inward religion*, the only true ground uniting the invisible community of believers.

This distinction opened the way to a "secular" conception of the relationship between State and Church, in which the State would have control over the signs of outward religion, in the interests of public order, but would be forbidden to interfere with inward religion, which was in any case beyond its reach.

By tradition and by conviction, the Regents' elite leaned towards Arminianism. The mathematicians, doctors and inventors who were making Holland a centre for modern science were drawn from this elite, men such as de Witt himself, Hudde and Huygens, who was perhaps the greatest of them all. These men of science were often ardent converts to Cartesianism, and they found that the theology of free will sat well with the demands of free intellectual research, a metaphysics of "clear and distinct ideas" and a rational conception of God. Some of them may even have gone further, tending towards a kind of religious scepticism, which married the naturalism of antiquity with the "scientific" politics then being expounded by their English contemporary Hobbes. At the centre of their preoccupations was the notion of a "natural right", which was the universal ground of morality and law, of trade and property. Whatever they may have believed precisely, the Regents' party agreed with the Remonstrants on two essential points: tolerance, as the condition of civil and religious peace, and thus of national unity; and the primacy of civil authority over the hierarchy of the Churches. This latter principle was also intended to prevent popular movements from establishing themselves in opposition to the State. It was to provide the subject for a series of theoretical writings, beginning with the *De Imperio Summarum Potestatum Circa Sacra* (Of the power of the Sovereign in religious matters) of Hugh de Groot (Grotius), which was published posthumously in 1647. The influence of de Groot's text can be seen quite clearly in Spinoza's work. It should nevertheless be noted that the *jus circa sacra* attributed to the State could be perfectly compatible with the practice of "private" forms of intolerance within its constituent communities.

On all these points, the Remonstrants were implacably at odds with the other Dutch Calvinists, the majority of their countrymen, known as *Contra-Remonstrants* or Gomarists (after Francis Gomar, Arminius's theological adversary in Leiden). The Gomarists were orthodox Calvinists. They maintained that all Christians owe a double allegiance: in temporal matters, to the magistrates or to the prince; in spiritual matters, to the Church. The Church should be totally independent of the State, with the absolute right to choose its own ministers, to assemble the faithful, to preach and to teach. But if the citizen owes a double allegiance, the law itself proceeds from the one source of all authority: God himself. It is part of a single divine plan for salvation. It defines one "Christian society", and one only, of which the Church and the State are only ever imperfect approximations. This explains why their relationship is not symmetrical: for the temporal ruler has an absolute right to the obedience of his subjects only if he is indeed a "Christian prince", zealous to ensure that the true faith is disseminated throughout the nation. In practice, then, the pastors who came out of the universities insisted that municipal and State authorities should keep a close eye on those heresies that lay in wait for their flock, who were the People of God, the new Israel. Thus a religious denomination that in other contexts was at the centre of resistance to absolutism came to exercise an essentially repressive function in Holland. And yet, despite this, the Gomarist movement still provided a focal point for the expression of the aspirations of the common people. The rural poor and the urban proletariat were both predominantly Calvinist. So were the petty bourgeoisie, amongst whom the Contra-Remonstrants recruited their pastors, young men ambitious to direct the conscience of the masses. These "preachers" denounced not only the theological laxity of the Regents but also their opulent way of life and their stranglehold on public affairs. In this way, their preaching even came to contain a "democratic" element.

Yet Arminianism was not the only enemy of orthodoxy, which found itself confronted by many other "heresies", in particular those which looked to a "second Reformation". These movements can be loosely grouped together under the name given them by Leszek Kolakowski, the "Christians without a Church". Behind this simple phrase lurks a multiplicity of different groups, who disagreed with each other on many articles of faith. What united them was their insistence on the interiorisation, and thus the individualisation, of faith. Most of them shared the Arminians' belief in free will and their rejection of predestination. Some of them had mystical tendencies; others, on the contrary, were close to a form of "natural religion". The Socinians (followers of Faustus Socinus, the Italian reformer who lived in Poland and whose name was enough to instil fear in orthodox theologians throughout classical Europe) held the doctrines of the Trinity and of original sin to be superstitions that the Church had imposed on the unity of the divine being. This movement prepared the ground from which the Unitarian or anti-Trinitarian sects were to spring. From this perspective, Christ was no longer a divine person, but an allegory of the moral virtues and of inward perfection. His function as the redeemer of humanity was thus stripped of its significance. A streamlined theology of this kind, from which the great "mysteries" of faith had been cut away, could easily be combined with a rationalistic philosophy of Cartesian inspiration (though we should remember that Descartes himself was a devout Roman Catholic).

Many of the "Christians without a Church" were nevertheless seduced by messianic themes, which proclaimed the advent of the kingdom of freedom and of divine justice, and they sought to decipher signs of their vision's imminent realisation in contemporary events, such as the conversion of the Jews. Those communities that belonged to the Anabaptist tradition (the Mennonites and the Collegiants, for instance) were organised on the evangelical model, as free assemblies of believers, without any ecclesiastical hierarchy. This was another kind of democratic tendency, which grew up in opposition to the Calvinists but also came to influence some of the same social groups. Some Anabaptists, in particular the Collegiants, held that the same organisational model should be applied to civil society. They denied that the State had the right to order its subjects to break the commandment "Thou shalt not kill", and they looked forward to an egalitarian society, founded on a communism of work and love for one's neighbour.

In 1619, the Synod of Dort had condemned the Arminian theses and forbidden pastors who professed them to minister to the faithful. The polemic that surrounded this decision did not die away: Arminians continued to play a leading role in the intellectual life of the country, debating with scholars and theologians from other denominations (as well as with Jews, amongst them Menasseh ben Israel, one of the young Spinoza's masters). The orthodox pastors were all the more vigilant as the execution of the Synod's directives had been left to the municipal authorities and in many towns a de facto tolerance reigned. It seemed that by 1650 Arminianism had carved out a place for itself in the life of the Dutch State. The freedom of publication that reigned in Amsterdam, and which had no equivalent elsewhere at that time, served to foster an atmosphere of free-thinking and tolerance. The Anabaptist "sects", the Quakers who had come there from England and various millenarian groups took full advantage of these freedoms, and their vigorous activity not only irritated the theologians but also unsettled the political authorities.

As early as 1610, the princes of Orange had declared themselves the protectors of the Calvinist Church, in an act of calculation rather than conviction (wasn't The Hague worth a sermon?). Since then, they had continuously used the Church's influence to put pressure on the Regents' party. Meanwhile, although Gomarism was above all committed to achieving its own doctrinal aims, it had nevertheless chosen to support the monarchist tendency against the "stadholderless Republic". On both sides, this alliance corresponded to a tactical decision rather than to any real community of thought. But it was all the more necessary as the mass of the common people tended towards a strict Calvinism and – at least in moments of crisis – usually put their trust in the princes rather than the Regents, whom they suspected of placing their own individual interests before those of the nation. The result was a rather complicated configuration of allegiances, which can be represented, with some simplification, as follows:

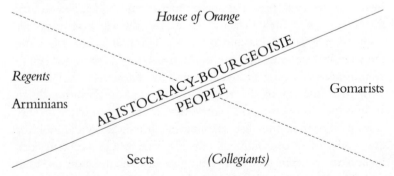

How can we "locate" Spinoza the individual and his thought within this complex, mobile topography? The Portuguese Jewish community in Amsterdam, into which he was born, was closely

associated with the commercial and colonial activities that constituted the power base of the governing elite of Holland. His own
father was a senior figure in that elite. Following his "excommun-
ication" in 1656, he was taken up by the enlightened sections of
the petty bourgeoisie and in particular by Collegiant and Cartesian
groups. It was from these groups that his "circle" of friends was
drawn, right up to the time of his death. Under the influence of
his philosophy, which they interpreted as an "ultra-Cartesian"
rationalism, or even as straightforward atheism, some of his friends
came to adopt radical positions. One in particular, Adriaan Koerbagh, was convicted of impiety and sentenced in 1668. It was
probably his death in prison that made Spinoza decide to publish
the *TTP* anonymously. At the same time, other relationships,
stemming in the first instance from his scientific researches, brought
him into the immediate sphere of the Regents' party. It would
even seem that he was, in some sense, an unofficial "adviser" to
Johan de Witt.

What is clear, with the benefit of hindsight, is that the philosophical demands made upon Spinoza by those around him brought
together three very different kinds of expectation. Even if these
different demands were sometimes made by the same men, they
remained fundamentally heterogeneous, corresponding to the
imperatives of science, of non-denominational religion and of
republican politics. Not only was Spinoza aware of these various
demands, but he displaced each of them in turn, never responding
to any of them according to the expectations that lay behind them.

The *TTP* is pervaded by a sense of urgency. There is an urgent
need to reform philosophy so as to eliminate, from within,
theological prejudice, "the relics of man's ancient bondage" (*TTP*,
22). There is an urgent need to defend philosophy against the
forces that threaten its free expression. There is an urgent need to
analyse the reasons for collusion between the principle of monarchical authority and religious fundamentalism, which has mobilised
the "multitude" against the interests of the nation and therefore
against their own interests. There is also an urgent need to
understand the kind of life that fosters those feelings of impotence
in which the spurious "second nature" of theological illusions has
its origin. If we can do this, then we should be in a position to see
freedom, both inward and outward, individual and collective, not

as a threat to our security, but as that security's fundamental condition.

There can be no doubt which "camp" Spinoza belonged to, if we accept that, in the historical context in which the *TTP* was written and published, naming the "enemy" is a clear and irrefutable sign. His "theological-political" intervention belongs to a tradition which dates back at least as far as Grotius: it is a manifesto for the Republican party. But it is not a manifesto that would give much comfort to those whom it was supposed to support. Spinoza knew who his enemy was. But that does not mean that he was prepared to accept the current Republican ideology and defend the interests of its supporters, any more than he was prepared to identify himself with the interests and ideology of the scientists or the "Christians without a Church". Indeed, how could he do so when these different positions did not converge in any coherent way? In a sense, the real "freedom party" was still to be created. The different elements that would make up its creed could be found scattered about in different places, but there were no obvious lines of agreement along which to join them together. Was this impression simply a misunderstanding which theory could easily rectify? Spinoza implicitly projects the model of a way of life and a form of social conscience that would marry the egalitarianism of the multitude *and* the construction of a State capable of guaranteeing their security, the religion of inward certainty *and* rational knowledge of the chain of natural causes. Is this model simply a fantasy? Had he formulated a set of principles which allowed him to transcend the weaknesses and inherent contradictions of bourgeois Republicanism as they were illustrated by the Regents' class? Or was he merely trying to preserve a historic compromise, for which it was already too late? These are the questions we must now address.

2

THE *TRACTATUS THEOLOGICO-POLITICUS*: A DEMOCRATIC MANIFESTO

The difficulty – and the interest – of the political theory set out in the *TTP* lies in the tension it creates between notions which are apparently incompatible and which are still perceived as such even today. This tension at first appears to stem from the attempt to transcend the ambiguities inherent in the idea of "tolerance". In order to determine what is at stake here, I shall begin by examining the relationship between the sovereignty of the State and individual freedom. This will lead me, on the one hand, to question the thesis that democracy has its basis in "nature" and, on the other, to discuss the Spinozist conception of history and its novel method of classifying political regimes into three categories: theocracy, monarchy and democracy.

Freedom of Thought and the Right of the Sovereign

The sovereignty of the State is always *absolute*. If it were not absolute, it could not claim to be sovereign. Individuals, according to Spinoza, cannot withdraw their active participation from the State to which they belong without finding themselves classed as "public enemies", with all the risks that entails (cf. chapter XVI). Yet at the same time, any State that wishes to guarantee its own stability must allow the individuals who live in it the greatest possible freedom of thought and of self-expression (cf. chapter XX). How can these two theses be reconciled? One seems to derive from an absolutist, not to say totalitarian, conception of the State, while the other is apparently the expression of a fundamental democratic principle. Spinoza himself provides the answer to this question at the very end of his book: the two theses can be made to fit together by applying a *fundamental rule* which rests upon the distinction between thoughts and words on the one hand, and actions on the other.

> Thus the purpose of the state [*Respublica*] is, in reality, freedom. Furthermore, we have seen that the one essential feature in the formation of the state was that all power to make laws should be vested in the entire citizen body, or in a number of citizens, or in one man. For since there is a considerable diversity in the free judgment of men, each believing that he alone knows best, and since it is impossible that all should think alike and speak with one voice, peaceful existence could not be achieved unless every man surrendered his right to act just as he thought fit. Thus it was only the right to act as he thought fit that each man surrendered, and not his right to reason and judge. So while to act against the sovereign's decree is definitely an infringement of his right, this is not the case with thinking, judging, and consequently with speaking, too, provided one does no more than express or communicate one's opinion, defending it through rational conviction alone, not through deceit, anger, hatred, or the will to effect such changes in the state as he himself decides. For example, suppose a man maintains that a certain law is against sound reason, and he therefore advocates its repeal. If he at the same time submits his opinion to the judgment of the sovereign power (which alone is competent to enact and repeal laws), and meanwhile does nothing contrary to what is commanded by that law, he deserves well of the state, acting as a good citizen should do. But if on the contrary the purpose of his action is to accuse the magistrate of injustice and to stir up popular hatred against him, or if he seditiously seeks to repeal that law in spite of the magistrate, he is nothing more than an agitator and a rebel. (*TTP*, 293)

This rule will create many problems. To begin with, there are problems of interpretation. We must bear in mind what Spinoza has already said in chapter XVII on the subject of obedience. Obedience does not lie in the motive from which one acts, but in the conformity of the act itself. "From the fact . . . that a man acts from his own decision, we should not forthwith conclude that his action proceeds from his own right, and not from the right of the government" (*TTP*, 251). In this sense, the State is the *supposed* author of all actions that conform to the law, and all actions that are not against the law can be said to conform to the law. Next, there is a problem of application: as Spinoza himself demonstrates, *certain words are actions*, in particular those which deliver judgements on the policy of the State and which may serve to obstruct that policy. It is therefore necessary to determine "to what extent this freedom can and should be granted" (*TTP*, 292), or again "which political beliefs are seditious" (*TTP*, 294). The answer to these questions does not depend only on a general principle of the following type: exclude those opinions which, implicitly or explicitly, tend to dissolve the social covenant, that is, which call for a "change in the form" of the State that might endanger the State's existence. It also depends on whether or not the State itself is "corrupt". Only in a healthy State can this rule, which will help to preserve the State, be unequivocally applied. But this leads us to a third problem: that of the theoretical meaning of Spinoza's thesis.

Let us begin by eliminating one apparently obvious interpretation: that the distinction proposed by Spinoza simply reproduces the distinction between *the private* (opinions) and *the public* (actions). In the liberal tradition, political sovereignty and individual freedom operate in these two separate spheres. They do not normally overlap but reciprocally "underwrite" each other. In this framework one can then resolve such conflicts as that between political and religious authorities, in the form of a "separation of Church and State". But this approach, which was soon to be developed by Locke, is clearly not that of Spinoza. For it ascribes *too little* "right" *both* to the individual *and* to the State. The individual is thus unduly limited, because the essential area in which he should be able to exercise his freedom of opinion is the area of politics itself. The State is unduly limited too, because its control should extend, directly or indirectly, to all the different relationships that may exist between men, and thus to all their actions, including acts of religious devotion. Experience shows that men's behaviour towards their "fellow citizens" or "neighbours" is always influenced by their religious opinions. Even if the distinction between the public and the private is a necessary institution of the State (*TTP*, 244), it cannot be one of its constitutive *principles*. So the rule put forward by Spinoza cannot imply a straightforward separation. In fact, what Spinoza wants to prove is a much stronger thesis (and a much riskier one too): that the sovereignty of the State and individual freedom do not need to be separated, nor indeed conciliated, because they are not in contradiction. *The contradiction lies precisely in the attempt to set them up in opposition to one other.*

Spinoza does not deny that the possibility of conflict exists between these two terms. But it is out of this very tension that a workable solution must emerge. This can be seen, for instance, if we consider what happens when the State tries to suppress freedom of opinion: "let it be supposed that this freedom can be suppressed and that men can be kept under such control that they dare not whisper anything that is not commanded by the sovereign" (*TTP*, 295). Such a policy, however, would necessarily be the ruin of the State itself, not because it is inherently unjust or immoral, but because it is physically unbearable:

> Men in general are so constituted that their resentment is most aroused when beliefs which they think to be true are treated as criminal, and when that which motivates their pious conduct to God and man is accounted as wickedness. In consequence, they are emboldened to denounce the laws and go to all lengths to oppose the magistrate, considering it not a disgrace but honourable to stir up sedition and to resort to any outrageous action in this cause. Granted, then, that human nature is thus constituted, it follows that laws enacted against men's beliefs are directed not against villains but against men of good character [*ingenui*], and their purpose is to provoke honourable men rather than to restrain the wicked. Nor can they be enforced without great danger to the state [*imperium*]. (*TTP*, 296)

The more violent the constraints that are placed upon individual freedom, the more violent and destructive will be the reaction against them. This is a "law of nature". When each individual is in some sense obliged to *think like another*, the productive force of his thought becomes a destructive force instead. This leads, in the extreme case, both to a sort of raving madness on the part of the individuals and to the perversion of all social relations. This contradiction is obviously all the more acute when the State is identified with a religion, either because civil authority has been annexed by religious authority, or because it forces on the individual a "world view" that seeks to displace religion and is thus, whatever its intention, of the same nature as a religion. Such a system could only last if all the individuals concerned were indeed able to believe in the same God in the same way and in the same terms. But such uniformity is not only impossible, it is inconceivable. In every society, barbaric or civilised, Christian or "idolatrous", opposing opinions about divinity, piety and morality, nature and the human condition are perpetually emerging. This is so because men's opinions are, for the most part, a product of the imagination, and the imagination of each individual (the stories he puts together, the images he projects onto the world) depends irreducibly on his own "complexion" – what Spinoza calls, using a term that has no direct equivalent in English, his *ingenium* (which we might translate as "nature" or "temperament"). By *ingenium*, we should understand (drawing on the account of individuality in the *Ethics*, IIP10–36) a memory whose form has been determined by the individual's experience of life and by his various encounters, and which, as a result of the unique way in which it has been constituted, is inscribed both in the mind (or soul) and in the dispositions of the body. For the opinions of individuals all to be reducible to a single world view, it would be necessary not only that they should all desire the same thing, but that they should have had the same experiences; in short, that they should be strictly indistinguishable from one another. This, of course, is a contradiction in terms.

Thus the ideologically repressive State will have an ineluctable tendency to destroy itself. But Spinoza takes his argument further, to its most radical conclusion. The same, he says, is true for the State that allows an ideological centre of opposition to develop, as history has shown many times: the struggle between the kings and the high priests among the ancient Hebrews; the struggle between the Roman Church and the Empire in mediaeval Europe; and most recently the struggle which raged between the English monarchy and the Protestant sects. For, as we have already pointed out, it is the very same individuals, each with his own *ingenium*, or more precisely it is the very same actions, "just" or "unjust", "pious" or "impious", that fall under the two precepts of obedience to the State and obedience to the divine law. A single territory – that occupied by the "community" of men – cannot support two sovereign powers at the same time. This explains why the Churches seek to organise themselves on the model of the State, as a "state within the state" (*imperium in imperio*) (*TTP*, 270; translation modified), while their leaders assume, by right or by force, a political function. This situation will, ultimately, lead to the dissolution of the State. But it carries no advantage for the individual, who finds himself transformed into the instrument of a rivalry over which he has no control. Nothing is more unlikely and more miserable than a man struggling to think in total isolation from other men. But nothing is more intolerant than a power which in order to defeat its rival is obliged to manipulate the credulity, the fears and the hopes of men.

It is at this point that Spinoza moves from a purely negative argument to a positive one. For if the State can survive neither by imposing opinions on individuals nor by tolerating an autonomous, organised centre of spiritual authority and opposition, if both these situations are virtually intolerable for the individuals who live under them, then there is only one possible solution.

This solution supposes first that the State reserves for itself absolute rights over religious practice – *jus circa sacra* – and delegates those rights to the Churches only to the extent that it can control the use that is made of them. In fact, "religion can acquire the force of law only from the decree of those who have the right to command, and . . . God has no special kingdom over men save through the medium of those who hold the sovereignty" (*TTP*, 281). But such an absolute sovereignty sanctions, by this very fact, the distinction between *inward* religion and *outward* religion: for it establishes the sovereign as "the interpreter of the divine law" (*TTP*, 283; translation modified) while forbidding him, in his own interests, to prescribe or make official any "opinions", that is, any models of thought and of virtue, besides the "common notions" of charity and justice towards our fellow men. In these conditions, if the isolated Churches and communities of faith appear to be autonomous, that is because there is an implicit de facto consensus on fundamental values, which is all the more effective for being implicit, and through which citizens will feel themselves to be "urged by love" rather than "driven by fear of a threatened evil" (*TTP*, 251).

This initial liberation will, in practice, condition all those that are to follow. On this basis, the State must open up of its own accord the largest possible domain for the expression of individual opinions. The "complexion" of each individual will then no longer be seen as an obstacle to the sovereign's power (*potestas*), but as an active, constitutive element of the power (*potentia*) of the State. When individuals consciously take part in the construction of the State, they naturally desire both its power over them and its preservation. By promoting freedom of opinion, the State maximises its chances of reaching rational decisions; at the same time, it places the individual in a situation in which obedience is the only form of conduct he can choose that is truly to his advantage. It is then that *thoughts and words are once more actions*, in the strongest sense of the term. And if it is necessary for individuals to obey any given law, even if it is an absurd law (for the danger that would result from disobedience is always greater than that which would stem from an error or act of madness on the part of the sovereign) (*TTP*, 241–2), it is even more important for the State to encourage the expression of all opinions, even those which are absurd or dangerous, for their utility far outweighs the inconvenience caused by their expression. Envisaged from a non-formal perspective, sovereignty as it actually exists turns out to be a continuous process of collective production in which individual powers are "transferred" to the public authority and ideological fluctuations are stabilised. Speech is one moment in this process. The *limit* implied by the existence of a State (the subordination of acts to the law and the banning of "subversive" opinions) expresses nothing other than the effectiveness of the process by which the State is constituted.

Democracy: "The Most Natural" State

The effectiveness of this process of reciprocal limitation increases in proportion as each of the two terms – the State and the individual – "interiorises" the utility of the other. In this way, the fantasy of unlimited power is replaced by a maximum of real power (Spinoza speaks in this context of "moderation", *TTP*, 292). It is therefore a form of *self-limitation*. Employing a fundamental category of the Spinozist metaphysic, we can say that the process of self-limitation expresses a causality that is immanent to the construction of the State.

The reader, however, cannot avoid coming up against the question, Is this argument valid for *every State* (for the State "in general")? Or is it in fact implicitly determined by the hypothesis of a *democratic* State? The negative argument (violence exerted against diversity of opinion undermines the State itself) is clearly of universal application. But the positive argument (the expression of diverging opinions reveals the common interest and is the means through which the power of the State is constructed) would seem to apply only to a democracy, in which the sovereign is none other than the totality of thinking individuals:

> Therefore, without any infringement of natural right, a community can be formed and a contract be always preserved in its entirety in absolute good faith according to this rule [*ratio*], that everyone transfer all the power that he possesses to the community, which will therefore alone retain the sovereign natural right over everything, that is, the supreme rule [*imperium*] which everyone will have to obey either of free choice or through fear of the ultimate penalty. Such a community's right is called a democracy, which can therefore be defined as a united body of men which corporately possesses sovereign right over everything within its power. (*TTP*, 241)

But isn't Spinoza's thinking on this point dangerously circular? First of all, there is a theoretical circle: the democratic State only appears as ultimately the most stable because from the very beginning implicitly democratic postulates have been built into the definition of the State in general. Then there is a practical circle: undemocratic States, which are those most ignorant of the fact that power and freedom necessarily imply one another, would seem in this analysis to have little chance of mastering their own arbitrary natures and thus escaping dissent, revolt and revolution, though they are most in need of being saved from this fate. On the other hand, a State that could plausibly make a rational calculation as to the benefits of freedom and thus preempt the violence that ideological censorship would provoke is inevitably a State that already operates according to this principle. In the political perspective which, as we have seen, is that of Spinoza, such a circular argument would leave only a very restricted margin for intervention in times of crisis: one could try and correct an aberration that had not yet gone too far, a momentary divergence between the democratic essence of the "free Republic" and the faults of its praxis. But one could not do much more. This might help to explain the pathetic tone of certain passages in the *TTP* which seem to express the fear that it might already be too late, that the republican "form" may already have been secretly occupied by a different content (*TTP*, 161, 220–1).

This is a real difficulty. Without playing on the inherent ambiguity of the word *nature* (which at times necessarily includes the idea of violence and at other times stands in opposition to it), it is difficult to maintain both that all existing forms of the State are the result of natural causes and that democracy is "the most natural State" (*TTP*, 297). In chapter XVI ("The basis of the state [*respublica*]; the natural and civic right of the individual; and the right of sovereign powers"), Spinoza seems to have come up against this problem directly, judging by the way his text wavers between a definition of the State in general (or a description of the "origins" of any civil society) and an analysis of the forms specific to democracy. It is as if the concept of democracy were being given a double theoretical inscription. On the one hand, it is a particular kind of political order, which results from determinate causes. But it is also the "truth" of every political order, in relation to which the internal consistency, causes and ultimate tendencies of their constitutions can be assessed.

This theoretical privilege of democracy is expressed through the closely interlinked usage of the concepts of the "social covenant" and of "reason". Every civil society can be considered as the outcome of a pact, whether "tacit or explicit". It is rational to try to escape from the poverty and insecurity of the "state of nature", in which men are guided exclusively by their particular appetites and desires. Indeed, "it is a universal law of human nature that nobody rejects what he judges to be good except through hope of a greater good or fear of greater loss, and that no one endures any evil except to avoid a greater evil or to gain a greater good" (*TTP*, 239). Democracy reveals the mechanism that is present in every such pact: individual powers are either "pooled" or transferred *en bloc*, so as to create a structure of civil obedience. And it is through such obedience that reason becomes a practical principle:

> in a democracy there is less danger of a government behaving unreasonably, for it is practically impossible for the majority of a single assembly, if it is of some size, to agree on the same piece of folly. Then again, as we have shown, it is the fundamental purpose of democracy to avoid the follies of appetite and to keep men within the bounds of reason, as far as possible, so that they may live in peace and harmony. (*TTP*, 242)

Thus democracy appears as a demand that is immanent in every State. This thesis may be logically problematic, but its political

meaning is plain. Every State institutes reciprocal forms of domination and obedience, through which individuals are made *subject
to* an objective order. But the condition of the subject is not the
same as that of a slave, and a generalised slavery does not constitute
a State. The concept of the State includes both the *imperium* and
the *respublica*. In other words, the condition of the subject presupposes *citizenship*, in the sense of activity (and therefore an equality
which is deemed to be proportional to that activity). This activity
finds its fulfilment in the democratic State, where "nobody transfers
his natural right to another so completely that thereafter he is not
to be consulted; he transfers it to the majority of the entire
community of which he is a part", so that "all men remain equal,
as they were before in a state of nature" (*TTP*, 243). The consent
on which the real power of a State depends always *tends* towards
this maximal adequation of form and content. The form may
remain passive, but there will always be a minimal element of
activity in the content, that which inscribes and expresses the
interests of the individuals concerned. Even before sovereignty can
be defined as the "sovereignty of the people", a "people" already
exists, irreducible to a multitude of plebeians or a passive mob.

This explains how the "theoretical" and "practical" attributes of
sovereignty, which seemed to be in contradiction with each other,
are to be held together.

- the sovereign power is bound by no law (*TTP*, 241);
- the welfare of the people is the highest law, to which all other
  laws, both human and divine, must be made to conform (*TTP*,
  284);
- it is exceedingly rare for governments to issue quite unreasonable
  commands; in their own interest and to retain their rule, it
  especially behoves them to look to the public good and to
  conduct all affairs under the guidance of reason. For, as Seneca
  says, "violenta imperia nemo continuit diu" – no-one who relies
  upon violence can govern for long (*TTP*, 242);
- I grant that the sovereign can by right govern in the most
  oppressive way and execute citizens on the most trivial pretexts,
  but no one will claim that by doing so they are acting in
  accordance with the judgement of sound reason. Indeed, since
  they cannot so act without endangering the whole fabric of the

state, we can even argue that they do not have the absolute power to do so, and consequently that they do not have the absolute right to do so. For we have demonstrated that the right of sovereigns is determined by their power (*TTP*, 292).

The "strength" of a State, whatever kind of State it may be, is defined by its capacity to endure, while preserving the form of its institutions. But once its citizens actively begin to ignore the commands of the sovereign, the seed of its dissolution has been sown. Therefore, in concrete terms, a strong State is one in which the subjects never disobey those rulings that the sovereign decrees to be in the general interest, in peacetime as in war (*TTP*, 244–6). But this definition is only meaningful when we know *in what conditions* such a result can practically be achieved. If it does not answer this question, then even the best political theory is only a work of fiction. "[T]he sovereign right over all men is held by him who holds the supreme power whereby he can compel all by force and coerce them by threat of the supreme penalty, universally feared by all," writes Spinoza. But he immediately adds, "[t]his right he will only retain as long as he has this power of carrying into execution whatever he wills; otherwise his rule will be precarious, and nobody who is stronger than he will need to obey him unless he so wishes" (*TTP*, 241). Further on, he declares, "sovereign powers possess the right of commanding whatever they will only for as long as they do in fact hold supreme power. If they lose this power, with it they also lose the right of complete command, which passes to one man or a number of men who have acquired it and are able to retain it" (*TTP*, 242).

This idea is both powerful and paradoxical, The absolute character of sovereignty is a de facto truth. Revolutions are by definition illegal and illegitimate (even to conceive one is a crime: *TTP*, 245–6) – until they have succeeded! But once they have taken place, and a new power has been established, a new authority is thereby created which is no less – and no more – incontestable than that which preceded it. In effect, Spinoza is not so much proclaiming a "right of resistance" (against "tyrannical" regimes) as recognising, within the theory itself, that precarious regimes do collapse (above all those whose show of force is in fact a symptom of the provisional impotence of their subjects) and that legal systems serve to formalise an existing balance of power. But in that case, the maxim according to which "every state must preserve its own form of government" (*TTP*, 279; translation modified) cannot be presented as an unconditional principle. For it also has a practical ("prudential") meaning. It draws its validity from experience, which shows that, most often, the violent overthrow of a ruler or regime leads only to a situation that is just as bad as, if not worse than, that which went before. (Spinoza here cites the example of the English Commonwealth period.) Only in a State that was as free as possible, and which in this way reigned "over its subjects' hearts [*animus*]" (*TTP*, 251; translation modified), would this maxim be a necessary truth. But then it would simply be the normative expression of the natural consequence of that State's constitution.

A Philosophy of History?

The argument we have just examined draws on notions that were initially elaborated in relation to *nature*. Spinoza continually insists upon the fact that they constitute developments of "natural right", which he defines as equivalent to the power to act (*TTP*, 237ff.). In this sense, if there is a difference between the hypothetical condition of the isolated individual and the process of political construction – which one might represent as the passage from the state of nature to civil society – this difference does not correspond to an "exit" from the natural world into some other order, as it might for other theoreticians of natural right. For instance, it has nothing to do with an evolution from the animal order to the human order. The *same elements* are to be found in both situations. They have simply been redistributed according to the logic of an immanent causality.

One might think that for such a radical naturalism the notion of history would have no meaning. But in the *TTP* that is manifestly not the case. Rather, the "nature" with which we are dealing here is nothing other than a new way of thinking about history, according to a method of rational exegesis that seeks to explain events by their causes. In this respect, one could even say that in the *TTP* to know "God" adequately is, essentially, to know history immanently. Thus the theoretical language of "naturalism" can be translated at every point into the language of a theory of history. This becomes obvious when Spinoza turns the traditional question of the comparison between political regimes into a question about the tendency towards democracy that is inherent in any social order. But it can also be seen in his analysis of notions that have historical origins, such as *nation*: "nature creates individuals, not nations, and it is only difference of language, of laws, and of established custom that divides individuals into nations. And only the last two, laws and customs, can be the source of the peculiar character [*ingenium*], the particular mode of life, the particular set of attitudes that signalise each nation" (*TTP*, 267). The concept which is used here to differentiate between the individual's singularity and the singularity of a historically constituted group is *the same* as that which was earlier used to express the essence of the individual's singularity (*ingenium*). However, the fact that we have moved from one perspective to the other may help us establish the true importance of the difficulties that have so far arisen, even if it cannot resolve them definitively.

The elaboration of a historical discourse is far from being a neutral process, and a whole section of the *TTP* (chapters VII to X) is devoted to examining the conditions in which it may take place. At the centre of this discussion is the notion of *narrative*. Historical narrative is an essentially social form of writing. It draws on the imagination of the masses for its material, and its effects tend to be judged in terms of that imagination also. That is why a science of history must be a second-order narrative – as Spinoza would say, a "critical history" (*TTP*, 141, 161; translation modified).[1] It will take as its object both the necessary sequence of events, in so far as it can be reconstructed, and the way in which historical agents, who are for the most part unaware of the causes influencing their actions, imagine the "meaning" of their history. But such a method cannot be isolated from the context of its application. Throughout the *TTP*, Spinoza regularly takes on the role of historian in order to analyse the relationship between the way in which his contemporaries perceive their own history, and their supreme interpretative model, the great narrative of the destiny of Humanity, the Holy Scriptures. That is why he must

[1] Shirley translates this as "the historical study of Scripture". – TRANS.

tackle the problems of prophecy (chapters I–II), messianism (chapter III) and clericalism (chapters VII, XII). These arguments, as we shall see, provide him with comparative elements which help him to understand what, in the life of a people, is substantially repetitive, and what, on the contrary, is irreversible. If all the different aspects of this inquiry culminated in a single, unambiguous explanatory schema, then we could say that what Spinoza has constructed is a philosophy of history. The situation we are confronted with, however, is rather more complex.

The principal constituent of Spinoza's analyses is what we might call, following Alexandre Matheron, a historical theory of the "passions of the body social". A new dimension of the political problematic, which had hitherto remained implicit, now emerges forcefully: the *movement of the masses* as a determining factor in the destiny of the State (cf. in particular chapters XVII and XVIII).

"The Hebrew State ... might have lasted indefinitely", if we are to judge by the formal perfection of the mechanisms of obedience and social cohesion with which it was endowed by Moses (*TTP*, 272). But the important point is that it did not, nor can any other State. The dissolution of the State may not occur at a date that can be determined in advance, but it is certainly not accidental. Even when it is the result of an "encounter" with a more powerful external enemy, the ultimate explanation always lies in the development of internal antagonisms that have corrupted institutions and unleashed the passions of the masses (*multitudo*) (*TTP*, 49–51, 252, 275–7). As long as these antagonisms could still be reconciled, the Hebrew State was able to rise again, even after the worst disasters imaginable. It finally collapsed when antagonism degenerated into fanaticism. But where did these antagonisms spring from? From the institutions of the State themselves, in so far as the juxtaposition of powers created incompatible ambitions, authorised inequalities of right and of wealth, and identified justice and civic obedience with a way of life that refused all change and so was unable to satisfy human desire indefinitely. In this respect, our institutions are always ambivalent: in certain conditions they will correct their own internal weaknesses; in others, they will collapse, precipitating peoples and States into chaos and violence.

This inevitable instability in itself would not be enough to undermine the existence of a State (and thus of the nation it represents) if it were not for the fact that the whole of history is conditioned by the *fear of the masses*: both the fear they themselves feel and that which they inspire in others. A system of political institutions is, in the first place, a means of repressing the fear that stems from our awareness of chance and of violence. But it achieves this end only by recourse to fear itself, which is the basis of the authority of those who govern. Thus fear, instead of being eliminated, is merely displaced from one object onto another. Once this fear has become reciprocal, and those who govern, terrorised by the latent power of the masses, seek to terrorise them in turn (or to manipulate them so as to terrorise their rivals), a causal chain of violent passions (hatred between classes, parties and religions) is set in motion, which leads inevitably to civil war. The degeneration of political institutions, and the transformation of the people into a "ferocious multitude", no longer able to recognise its own true interest, are but two sides of the same coin. Tyranny forges the masses into an explosive combination of fear and revolutionary illusion. At the same time, their essential impotence and internal divisions make them yearn to be saved by a "man of providence". Yet there is every chance that such a man will turn out to be a tyrant, like Cromwell (*TTP*, 277–8).

This does not mean that the "law" governing history is necessarily the war of each against all, and that only the repressive power of the State prevents that war from breaking out at any moment. The excess of antagonistic passion is, essentially, a perversion of the desire to maintain and to safeguard the existing order. This desire is present even in fear itself, as can be seen by the fact that every fear is always accompanied by a hope (even if that hope has been diverted towards some purely imaginary object). In certain passages, Spinoza also seems to suggest that the existence of civil societies provides the conditions for progress in knowledge and in lifestyle – from "barbarism" to civilisation – within the history of each nation, and even across the history of humanity as a whole (*TTP*, 116–17, 272). By reducing general ignorance, this progress would weaken the grasp of fear and superstition, and thus calm the passions of the multitude. But this idea is merely a hypothesis.

The true problem of the *TTP* is that of the *meaning of Christianity*. It is obvious that Christianity did not "moralise" history, that is to say, that it did not at all alter the nature of the forces present in history. Rather, it introduced an additional force – itself – into the natural scheme of social antagonisms (*TTP*, chapter XIX). The birth of Christianity does not correspond to the honouring of a promise, nor to an intervention of Providence. Yet it nevertheless determined, retrospectively, a decisive break in human history. Why was that?

What is enigmatic – but not "mysterious" – about the person of Christ himself, is his extraordinary ability to "commune [*communicare*] with God, soul to soul" (*TTP*, 65; translation modified). He is able to perceive the commandment to love one's neighbour as a universal truth and to express it not in the language of a single nation or a single individual "complexion", but in a language made up of "beliefs and doctrines held in common by all mankind" (*TTP*, 107). Yet Christ's knowledge is not, for all that, limitless. Faced with the ignorance and resistance of the people, he too confused the language of necessity with the language of the law (*TTP*, 108). To understand all these aspects of his teaching, we must remember that, like certain prophets whose teaching prefigured his (such as Jeremiah), he lived during a period in which the State was falling apart (*TTP*, 146–7, 283–8). There was a total lack of public security and solidarity. He therefore had to draw on the biblical tradition (which was intimately bound up with the history of the Hebrew nation and their State) and extract from it those moral teachings that can be shared by all human beings. These he presented as a divine universal law which is addressed to each of us individually, "privately". However profoundly true this idea of Christ's was, it carried with it an abstract, fictional element: that religion concerned "men as men", not only in their likeness to each other, but abstracted from any political relationship and living as if "in the state of nature". It is this fictional element that allows the truth to be perverted. The commandment of universal charity (every man is my neighbour) is transformed into a commandment of humility (love your enemy, "turn the other cheek"). This perversion can even take the form of a straightforward inversion, as it did with the first disciples of Christ, Paul in particular. They lived in a period of political crisis of an even greater scale than that which their master had known – the crisis of the Roman Empire, which for them represented the whole of the civilised world. Their response was to codify this idea of a "law" that is independent of the existence of any civil society and thus superior to any existing law (*TTP*, 212–13, 295–6). They gave this law a spiritualist content (the condemnation of the "flesh"), which they legitimated by deifying the person of Christ. This led directly to a third stage, in which it became possible to use the teaching of Christ *against* historical States by constructing a "universal Church", with its own apparatus of ceremony, dogma and ministers, and its own internal divisions (*TTP*, 118–21, 203). Just as the original error of Moses in granting the Levites a hereditary monopoly of the priesthood had weighed heavily on the history of the Hebrew State, so Christ's error would be paid for in the long term by a history of insoluble conflicts.

Yet despite or because of these contradictions, Christianity nevertheless constitutes an irrevocable turning point in the history of humanity, a cultural revolution whose effects reverberate still now. One essential indication of this is the fact that since Christ there have been no more prophets (*TTP*, 60, 196–204) – that is to say, no more men of exceptional virtue whose imaginations are so vivid they can represent both natural events and their own thoughts as "signs" from God, and can convey the proofs of their revelations to their fellow citizens, in order to reform behaviour and revive faith (*TTP*, chapters I and II). It is easy to see why this should be the case.

Every nation has had its prophets, but the vocation of the prophets of Israel was the result of a unique historical configuration. Moses had announced the divine law in the form of a command-ment accompanied by "terrifying" threats and by the promise of rewards, principally the prosperity of the nation itself (*TTP*, 84, 88–9, 113, 118, etc.). The law was identified exclusively with the right of the Hebrew nation and was materially inscribed on tablets that were kept in the Temple. Piety consisted, by definition, in rigorously observing the provisions of the law. Therefore, these provisions had to be comprehensible and could not surrender their power to constrain. The prophets acted as living mediators. They reminded the people in their own language of the existence of this law. They revived the threats and promises it contained through their interpretation of national history, and thus encouraged the Hebrews to choose obedience in their hearts (*animus*), particularly in times of trial when they may have found it hard to believe in

Israel's "election". Their function was a necessary one because of the *exteriority of the law*. As a result, the law had to be constantly revived and its meaning constantly demonstrated again in new situations, once the legislator who had brought them the law was no longer there to bear witness to his revelation. (In the *Ethics*, Spinoza will elaborate a theory of the superior force of present impressions over past impressions and of the "reinforcement" of the latter by the former: IVP 9–13.)

But with the preaching of Christ, this situation is reversed. Not only is the law now declared to all nations, not to one alone, but it is *internalised*, and as a result it is *always immediately available*. Christ did not conceive of revelation as the transmission of a physically audible message but as an intellectual illumination, and he inscribed that revelation "deep in our hearts" (*TTP*, 108; translation modified). Henceforth, the believer's task is not to go in search of external evidence for the divine promise, which would guarantee its permanence, but to discover within himself the present disposition of which Christ is the model, the inner signs of the "true life" (*TTP*, 218). Salvation will thus appear to him as a consequence of his virtue (which he may think of as an act of grace). And, as is immediately shown by the new style of preaching that characterised the mission of the Apostles (*TTP*, chapter XI), any questions he may have about the meaning of this revelation can only be answered by reasoned arguments that are accessible to human understanding, not by miracles that would contradict it. Thus every man is, in the last instance, his own mediator, and no man can truly act as a mediator of religion to others. For this reason, "every man is in duty bound to adapt these [universal] religious dogmas to his own understanding and to interpret them for himself in whatever way makes him feel that he can the more readily accept them with full confidence and conviction" (*TTP*, 225). Whoever then claims or believes himself to be a prophet must be a "false prophet". Nothing, however, makes it unthinkable that there should be other Christs.

The Legacy of Theocracy

Thus, though he does not organise them into a system, Spinoza sketches out in the *TTP* the main themes that structure his philosophy of history. It remains then to be asked, in what way do they modify our understanding of the problem of freedom? Do they provide us with a way to overcome the difficulties with which we were previously faced?

Even the best will in the world cannot remove the feeling of an underlying contradiction when confronted with certain passages of Spinoza's text. For instance, in chapter VII, Spinoza concludes his critique of the way in which the Churches and the philosophers have appropriated the Scriptures by explicitly ruling out any religious "high priesthood". Since true universal Religion

> consists in honesty and sincerity of heart rather than in outward actions, it does not pertain to the sphere of public law and authority.... Therefore, as the sovereign right to free opinion belongs to every man even in matters of religion, and it is inconceivable that any man can surrender this right, there also belongs to every man the sovereign right and supreme authority to judge freely with regard to religion, and consequently to explain it and interpret it for himself.... For since the supreme authority for the interpretation of Scripture is vested in each individual, the rule that governs interpretation must be nothing other than the natural light that is common to all, and not any supernatural [l]ight, nor any external authority. (*TTP*, 159–60)

Yet when we come to Spinoza's demonstration (in chapter XIX) that Religion only acquires the force of law (can only issue "commandments") through the decision of the Sovereign, he seems to be arguing for a position that is the reverse of the one he had previously defended:

> since it is the duty of the sovereign alone to decide what is necessary for the welfare of the entire people and the security of the state [*imperium*], and to command what it judges to be thus necessary, it follows that it is also the duty of the sovereign alone to decide what form piety towards one's neighbour should take, that is, in what way every man is required to obey God. From this we clearly understand in what way the sovereign is the interpreter of religion; and, further-more, we see that no one can rightly obey God ... unless he obeys all the decrees of the sovereign. For since we are bound by God's command to practise piety towards all men without exception and to harm no man, it follows that no one is permitted to assist anyone to another's hurt, far less to the detriment of the commonwealth

[*respublica*] as a whole. So no one can exercise piety towards his
neighbour ... nor obey God unless he obeys the decrees of the
sovereign in all things. (*TTP*, 284)

The sovereign alone is judge of the public good.

Certainly, one might argue that the first of these texts is dealing
with *inward religion*, or faith, and the second with *outward religion*,
or worship. But this in itself is not enough to remove the
contradiction, since the main issue at stake in both texts is that of
deeds (that is to say, "works" or "pious actions towards one's fellow
men") and this issue belongs at once to both domains. So we come
back to the fact that when the State imposes its own law, dictated
in the best cases by a concern for the "common welfare", on
outward religion, it is necessarily interfering with the performing
of works, and thus with faith itself, since "faith without works is
dead" (an idea nicely expressed by the notions of "justice and
charity"). Thus the unity that once existed between political
sovereignty and religious community is not, and never can be,
completely abolished. Indeed, its abolition could not be achieved,
even if *historical* Christianity were to be replaced by a "natural
religion" that delivered the same essential teaching, but was
independent of the *fact* of any revelation (*TTP*, 209–10, 212).

Thus Spinoza's conception of the relationship between the
religious and the political is apparently condemned to be "impure"
and unstable. We might express this idea by saying that although in
theory the perspectives of *nature* and *history* are identical, there is in
fact some distance between them. But might this not be precisely
the strong point of Spinoza's argument? For what if the contradiction was not in the first place a feature of the texts in which we
have located it, but a reality (which was itself historical) whose
analysis would require the invention of new methods and new
tools? It is this hypothesis I should now like to verify, by examining
the articulation of the concepts of theocracy, monarchy and
democracy. In the *TTP*, these three concepts take the place of
other, more traditional systems for the classification of political
regimes.

Spinoza did not invent the term *theocracy*. He borrowed it from
the classical historian Flavius Josephus, whose work constitutes the
principal non-biblical source for the history and institutions of the

Jewish people. Yet he does seem to have been the first writer to make systematic use of it, and he was certainly the first to forge from it a theoretical *concept*:

> [A]fter their departure from Egypt, the Hebrews were no longer bound by the laws of any other nation ... Finding themselves thus placed in this state of nature, they hearkened to Moses, in whom they placed the greatest confidence, and resolved to transfer their right not to any mortal man, but to God alone. Without much hesitation they all promised, equally and with one voice, to obey God absolutely in all his commands and to acknowledge no other law but that which he should proclaim as such by prophetic revelation. ... It was God alone, then, who held sovereignty [*imperium*] over the Hebrews, and so this state alone, by virtue of the covenant, was rightly called the kingdom of God, and God was also called the king of the Hebrews. Consequently, the enemies of this state were the enemies of God; citizens who aimed to seize the sovereignty were guilty of treason against God, and the laws of the state were the laws and commands of God. So in this state civil law and religion – which we have shown to consist only in obedience to God – were one and the same thing; the tenets of religion were not just teachings but laws and commands; piety was looked upon as justice, impiety as crime and injustice. He who forsook his religion ceased to be a citizen and by that alone became an enemy and a foreigner [*hostis*], and he who died for his religion was regarded as having died for his country. In short, there was considered to be no difference whatsoever between civil law and religion. Hence this form of government could be called a theocracy. ... (*TTP*, 254–5; translation modified)

The whole of chapter XVII develops this definition to provide a complete schema of the institutions of the Hebrew theocratic State, up to the establishment of the royal house. The schema deals not only with the State's theological-political structure, but also with its "economy" and its "social psychology". Spinoza concludes by deducing from it an explanation for the major trends of early Jewish history. Thus, on the one hand, "theocracy" defines a historically unique regime, apparently the only one of its kind. But this "singular essence" is also characterised by its long-term consequences for the history of the Jewish people and, more generally, by the effects it has disseminated throughout the history of humanity, through the mediation of Christianity. In this sense, one might hold that the legacy of theocracy, metaphorically speaking, lies in the impossibility for modern political societies to be entirely contemporaneous with themselves. They contain a kind of "delayed action mechanism", an inner displacement, which they cannot overcome. At the same time, we should note that there are several indications in Spinoza's text that he intended his analysis of theocracy to have a general significance. It represents a type (it is tempting to say an "ideal type") of social organisation, of behaviour on the part of the "multitude", and of the representation of power, whose equivalents, or at least approximations of them, can be found in many other kinds of State and in the political tendencies they represent. Perhaps they are to be found in *any* real State. This, then, explains the importance that, in the *TTP*, is given to elucidating the dialectic that defines theocracy.

In fact, what characterises the theocratic State is a profound contradiction. On the one hand, the Mosaic institutions represent the almost perfect realisation of a political unity. They achieve this in the first place through a subtle balance of powers and rights, which in practice produce a State that is already "self-limiting". (See, for example, their methods for appointing judges and military leaders, or for sharing religious authority between priests and prophets, or the rules which make rights of ownership in land inalienable.) Above all, though, they achieve this through the central principle of the State itself, which is the *identity of civil and religious law*. It is this identity which leads to the integral ritualisation of life, by which the individual is denied all possibility of doubt or deviation from his duty, and to the complete identification of individual and collective salvation. The election of the whole people of Israel conditions the love its citizens feel for one another. That is why the theory of theocracy is also a theory of nationalism as the most powerful affective resource of patriotism (*TTP*, 264–5).

It is true that all these features depend upon a certain "barbarism" or primitivism in Hebrew culture – Spinoza speaks of their "childishness" (*TTP*, 890).[1] This leads us to the other aspect of their extraordinary solidarity: the political culture of ritual obedience as a culture of superstition. Sovereignty can only be identified with divine authority by presupposing or imposing the perception that the whole of nature (and with it the realm of "chance") is a

---

[1] Shirley translates this as "immaturity". – TRANS.

goal-directed order created as such by God. The result is a culture of fear in its most uncontrollable form: fear of God, accompanied by an obsessive fear of impiety, from which flows a continual sadness. Theocracy is essentially sad. Solidarity, because it rests upon the identification of individuals, turns into its opposite – a menacing loneliness. Each man, fearing God's judgement at every moment, projects this anxiety onto the other, whose behaviour he observes, suspecting that it may bring down the wrath of God upon the community. Thus he comes to consider every "neighbour" a potential "enemy within". It then only remains for "theological hatred" to penetrate and pervade every conflict of opinion and ambition for those conflicts to become irremediable.

This contradiction can be explained if we see that theocracy, behind the apparent unity of its principles, in fact contains the seeds of two antithetical political tendencies. Spinoza had warned us from the start: "all this [the transfer of sovereign power to God alone] was a matter of opinion rather than fact" (*TTP*, 255; translation modified). This does not mean it was a pure fiction without any practical consequences. Rather, it means that in theocracy fiction itself determines praxis and acts as an immanent cause within reality. Its effects are therefore necessarily ambivalent. Thus, on the one hand, theocracy *is equivalent to democracy*: in handing over all power to God, the Hebrews were keeping it away from any particular man or men. They were all equally involved in their "alliance" with God, and despite their barbarism constituted themselves as citizens, fundamentally equal before the law and in regard of public office, patriotic duty and property rights. The Temple, "God's dwelling place", was their common house; it belonged to the whole people and symbolised their collective authority (*TTP*, 257). This imaginary method of establishing democracy is, perhaps, the only way in which it can begin to exist. But it supposes a figuration. It dramatises the displacement of collective sovereignty onto "another" stage. The *place of God (vicem Dei)* (*TTP*, 256; translation modified) must both be given a material form and left vacant if it is to house an authority that can transform the rules of social life into a set of sacred obligations. Can such a place be occupied by "no one"?

To begin with, it was occupied by Moses, as prophet-legislator speaking in the name of God, to whom the people voluntarily handed over all their powers. Later on, it remained "empty" but did not cease to exist: the various individuals who held civil and priestly office would turn to it in order to determine the grounds of their agreement and to confirm (or contest) their legitimacy before each other. Eventually, it will have to be occupied once more – at the request of the people themselves – by an individual who will be "the Lord's anointed", that is, *an individual who is at once both real and symbolic*. As a result, every historical monarchy contains an element of theocratic origin, which when translated yields the notion of the "divine right" of kings. The monarch, as an individual, possesses only an insignificant amount of power in comparison with the masses, and thus one monarch can easily be replaced by another. Moreover, since monarchs are mortal they are unable to guarantee the succession of their own line. That is why they profit from a revival of the memory of divine sovereignty, why they must demand an even more absolute obedience from their subjects, must turn the love and fear that they inspire into the love and fear of God, must appear before men as his representatives on earth, and must prevent any attempt to undermine superstition. But nothing can prevent rival representatives of God – usurpers, conquerors, high priests, prophets and reformers – from emerging in response to popular aspirations and rebellions.

Let us return, then, to democracy in the proper sense of the word. Is it true that, once individuals prove to be capable of exercising their collective sovereignty directly, without recourse to the fiction of an alliance with God (that is, without the imaginary displacement of that sovereignty) but through an explicit "social covenant", then the problem will have been completely resolved? Even without taking into account the superstition of the masses, this is manifestly not the case. The democratic State, constituted by the joint principles of the reciprocity of duties and the equality of rights, is governed by the will of the majority, which is the "sum" of all individual opinions. For this will to be imposed effectively, it is not enough for the sovereign to have the absolute right to command those actions that are in the public interest and the means to make sure his commands are carried out. There must also be a consensus that love of one's neighbour should outweigh personal ambition, that is, that one should "love one's neighbour as oneself". This is all the more necessary where freedom of opinion and expression are fully recognised as both the foundation and the purpose of the State. But, as we have seen, it would be both self-contradictory and ineffective to try and impose such a consensus by the authority of the State alone, depending as it does entirely on the "complexion" (*ingenium*) and the "heart" (*animus*) of each man. *It can only be brought about indirectly.* This is what will happen (or would happen) if, on the one hand, the State takes responsibility for the formal control of all religious rituals (and even undertakes to repress any excesses) and, on the other, individuals adopt the "dogmas" of "universal faith" (described by Spinoza in chapter XIV of the *TTP*) as the regulating principle of their beliefs and behaviour towards one another. In other words, they must subscribe to a "true Religion" in which Christianity tends to be identified with its essential moral teaching. Then God will be *represented nowhere* but he will *be everywhere*, "in the heart" of each individual, where he is practically indistinguishable from the effort to live a virtuous life.

Thus the two themes of the *TTP* – "true Religion" and the "natural right of the sovereign" – together with their correlatives – freedom of religious conscience and freedom of public opinion – are not one and the same. But together they form a necessary system. Each of them limits the other and protects it from the possibility of perversion. Each of them is the condition of the other's efficacy. Yet there is still a gap between the social "covenant" and the inner "divine law", even though the individual as believer is identical with the individual as citizen. In this space that separates them, there is no room to imagine a transcendent God. But there must be room for philosophy – or at least, for *a* philosophy. There must also be room for the desire of the multitude to live in a state of civil peace. But how can we be certain that two such different aspirations will prove compatible?

3

THE *TRACTATUS POLITICUS*:
A SCIENCE OF THE STATE

Spinoza began work on the *Tractatus Politicus* (*TP*), which was left unfinished at his death, only a few years after he had completed the *Tractatus Theologico-Politicus* (*TTP*). Yet the two books seem to belong to two entirely different worlds. The *TTP* had used long exegetical arguments and various strategies of persuasion to help its readers come to understand the causes of the crisis that loomed ahead of them and the means by which it might be averted. The *TP* has none of these. In their place is an exposition whose synthetic concision anticipates the "geometrical" approach of the *Ethics*, as it explicitly sets out to establish its argument according to rational principles. The result is a text that bears all the marks of scientific method.

It is not only the style that has changed. Both the logic of the theory that Spinoza advances and its political implications are significantly different from those of the earlier work. For the reader, these changes can be difficult to accept. There is, of course, a certain continuity, above all in the "definition" of natural right in terms of power (a theory to which Spinoza, as we shall see, now attributes a radical meaning.) The thesis put forward in the *TTP*, that freedom of thought lies beyond the reach of coercion and therefore falls outside the power of the sovereign, is restated here (*TP*, III, 8), though this freedom is no longer inseparably associated with the freedom to express one's opinions, or at least not explicitly so. However, what is most striking are the points not of continuity but of contrast. Spinoza no longer refers to the "social covenant" as a constitutive moment in the construction of civil society. Moreover, there is no mention of the thesis that "the purpose of the State is freedom", which was so forcefully present in the *TTP*, where it effectively functioned as the book's rallying cry. Instead, we have the following proposition: "the purpose of political order ... is simply peace and security of life" (*TP*, V, 2). Finally, despite several references to the analysis of religion presented in the *TTP*, the role of religion in politics is now clearly subordinate, if not marginal, and Spinoza's concept of the religious itself seems to have changed profoundly. There is only one allusion to "theocracy", which henceforth designates nothing more than one particular way of choosing a monarch (*TP*, VII, 25). Nor does the notion of "true Religion" figure in the *TP*. Instead, when discussing the aristocracy, Spinoza introduces the idea of a "religion of the homeland" (*TP*, VIII, 46),[1] which seems to refer back to the traditions of the cities of antiquity.

All these changes lead to a very different relationship between philosophy and history from that which obtained in the earlier book. Indeed, not even Spinoza's concept of history itself has survived intact. History is now subordinate to theory, for which it provides both a field of investigation and a source of illustrations. It is no longer the directional framework whose irreversible "moments" inscribe the constraints within which politics has to operate. Consequently, the Bible forfeits its former central role. "Sacred" history, even when rewritten from a critical perspective, can no longer claim to be a privileged source of political wisdom. Changes such as these cannot be reduced to the displacement of certain isolated concepts. Behind them lies an attempt to come to terms with a whole new order of philosophical problems.

After 1672: A New Order of Problems

Why has Spinoza's thought changed in this way? Doubtless, in part, because the *TP* is a work of a quite different genre. The *TTP* was a militant intervention in a contemporary polemic. It therefore had to take into account the questions posed and the language used by the parties with whom Spinoza was arguing. The *TP*, on the other hand, is presented as a work of theory, an inquiry into the "foundations of politics", unrestricted by any particular event or circumstances. These foundations were mentioned in the *TTP*,

---

[1] Wernham translates this as "state religion". – TRANS.

where it was stated that their full investigation would have to wait till later. In the *TP*, Spinoza certainly continues to claim that theory and practice (*praxis*) are inseparable, but he immediately adds – a thought lifted straight from Aristotle's *Politics* – that "every form of commonwealth [*civitas*] which can be devised to secure human concord, and all the means required to guide a people, or to keep it within definite bounds, have already been revealed by experience [*experientia*]" (*TP*, I, 3).

This argument, however, is too narrowly formal to be satisfactory. In my opinion, it serves to mask another, more decisive cause: the coincidence between the *internal difficulties of the TTP* (as sketched above) and a *historical event* which had occurred in the interim, namely the Orangist "revolution". In 1672, the Regents' party had been defeated, and mass violence had briefly erupted in the political life of the United Provinces. That Spinoza had these events in mind while writing the *TP* is apparent from the passages in which he discusses the causes that can bring about the dissolution of an aristocratic regime, a category he now took to include the Dutch Republic (*TP*, IX, 14; XI, 2). This historical context also informs the search for a means by which to "keep the multitude within bounds", a search that rapidly takes on the character of a veritable obsession (*TP*, I, 3; VII, 25; VIII, 4–5; IX, 14).

Is it possible to reconstruct the way in which Spinoza perceived these events from the content of his political theory? His first reaction to the murder of his friends and the fall of the regime that had previously seemed to him the best possible regime was one of grief and indignation. But once the moment of crisis began to recede, it was no longer clear that the "revolution" of 1672 did in fact bear out all the fears Spinoza had shared with other opponents of monarchism. Or if it did so, it was not in the form they had been expecting. To begin with, the prince of Orange proved himself capable of defending the nation successfully against the French invasion. In addition, the personal power he arrogated to himself was not institutionalised as a hereditary monarchy. The Regent class was forced to submit to the "dictatorship" of the military leader, but was not entirely deprived of power; rather, a compromise was reached. Lastly, it is true that the new regime did go some way towards satisfying certain of the Calvinists' demands in the matter of censorship. (It was in 1674 that the States officially banned the *TTP*, along with a work by Spinoza's friend, the Cartesian philosopher Louis Meyer, on the interpretation of Scripture, Hobbes's *Leviathan* and an anthology of the key texts of the Socinian "heresy". This selection seems to have covered the complete range of material that the orthodox pastors deemed to be dangerous to the faith. It was following this decree that Spinoza decided not to publish the *Ethics*.) But the resulting acts of censorship never amounted to the total subjugation of the State to the religious authorities. Instead, the immediate result of the steps which were taken was the disintegration of the deeply heterogeneous anti-Republican "front". The "theocratic" party saw its hopes frustrated. The governing classes first split, then regrouped around a new balance of power, which looked likely to prove as unstable as its predecessor.

In these circumstances, the question, where can true freedom be found? remained open. Indeed, it is a question that has to be asked anew for every historical regime – not as an unconditional question, but as a practical problem posed by the effects of that regime's mode of operation (*TP*, VII, 2; VII, 15–17; VII, 31; VIII, 44; X, 8, etc.). Not all regimes are the same in this respect, but no regime is formally incompatible with the affirmation of individuality, with what the *TP* calls a "truly human existence" (*TP*, V, 5). For each new regime, then, we have to determine the conditions of this compatibility. What is less clear, however, is how we should understand the notion of *absolutism* in this context.

Absolutism had long been an important subject of contemporary debate. At that period, in Holland as in France and England, the theoreticians of divine-right absolutism (such as Bossuet, who had studied the arguments of the *TTP* closely) were opposed by the partisans of a very different conception of absolute power. This alternative theory was inspired by the work of Machiavelli, who had already provided the "libertine" thinkers with the doctrine of the *raison d'Etat*. It is not by chance that the very first paragraph of the *TP* describes an antithesis between two types of political thought. One of these is denounced by Spinoza as "utopian" (after the title of Thomas More's celebrated book). This is the politics of the Platonic philosophers, who seek to derive the ideal constitution of the City from the Idea of the Good and from the hypothesis of a rational human nature, and who attribute the faults to be found in real constitutions to inherent "vices" or perversions. The other type of political thought is realistic (and, potentially at least, scientific). It is that of the "practitioners" and the "politicians", of whom Machiavelli is the archetype. Spinoza admits that Machiavelli's aims are far from clear but nevertheless defends him against his detractors and discusses his positions (*TP*, V, 7; cf. X, 1). He takes from him the idea that the value of institutions has nothing to do with either the virtue or the piety of individuals, but must be independent of all such conditions. This leads him to the following *fundamental rule*, which is stated several times in the course of the *TP*:

> when the safety of a state [*imperium*] depends on any man's good faith [*fides*], and its affairs cannot be administered properly unless its rulers choose to act from good faith, it will be very unstable; if a state is to be capable of lasting, its administration [*res publicae*] must be so organised that it does not matter whether its rulers are led by reason or passion – they cannot be induced to break faith or act badly. In fact it makes no difference to the stability of a state what motive leads men to conduct its affairs properly, provided that they are conducted properly. For freedom or strength of heart is a private virtue; the virtue of a state is stability. (*TP*, I, 6; translation modified)

> [I]f human nature were such that men desired most what was most useful to them, there would be no need of artifice to promote loyalty and concord. But since, it is well known, human nature is very different, it is necessary to organise the state [*imperium*] so that all its members, rulers as well as ruled, do what the common welfare requires whether they wish to or not; that is to say, live in accordance with the precept of reason, either spontaneously or through force or necessity. But this only happens when the administration is arranged so that nothing which concerns the common welfare is wholly entrusted to the good faith of any man (*TP*, VI, 3).

Should we deduce from statements such as these that Spinoza has adopted the anthropological pessimism to which Machiavelli's thought has traditionally been reduced ("Men are evil": *The Prince*, chapter 18)? We will return to this question later. The most urgent comparison, however, is that with Hobbes, whose two major works, the *De Cive* (1642) and the *Leviathan* (1651), had quickly gained a reputation in Dutch intellectual circles, where they were much discussed.

For Hobbes, the notions of "right" and "law" are in themselves antithetical, "like freedom and obligation". Man's natural right, that is, his originary individual freedom, is as such unlimited. But it is also self-destructive, for every right infringes all other rights, leading to a "war of each against all". As a result, the individual's very life is threatened. There is therefore an untenable contradiction, since the primary objective of the individual is his own survival. It is necessary then to go beyond this state of affairs. In order to establish a form of security, natural right must be replaced by civil right, that is, by a juridical order. Such an order can only be imposed by a higher force whose authority is absolutely beyond question. The state of nature (that is, of independent individuals) is thus replaced by an "artificial" individual, the "body politic", in which the will of the many is entirely *represented* by that of the sovereign (the law). By means of the "social contract", the individuals are held to have themselves instituted this representation. As a result, the body politic appears to be indivisible (for as long as it endures), just as the will of the sovereign is indivisible. Hobbes establishes (or re-establishes) the equivalence of power and right, but this equivalence *holds only for the sovereign himself*, to the exclusion of all private citizens, who are granted only areas of conditional freedom, of greater or lesser extent according to the requirements of the circumstances. It is true that these conditional freedoms always include the right to private property, which is guaranteed by the State as the major concession it makes in return for the power vested in it. Hobbes's absolutism, as this schematic overview shows, is founded on what has been called a "possessive individualism".[2]

In the 1660s, the theoreticians of the Dutch Republican party (among them Lambert de Velthuysen, one of Spinoza's correspondents: see *Letters* XLII–XLIII and LXIX) had used Hobbes's theory to combat both the idea of "divine right" and that of a balance of powers between the State and the body of municipal and provincial magistrates. This tactic was somewhat paradoxical, juridical absolutism being inseparable in Hobbes's thought from his support for monarchism. Only the singularity of the person of the sovereign can guarantee the unity of his will and thus the

---

[2] The classic exposition is that of C. B. Macpherson, *The Political Economy of Possessive Individualism: Hobbes and Locke* (Oxford: Clarendon Press, 1962). – ED.

indivisibility of the body politic that will preserve it from disintegrating into factions.

Spinoza, as we shall see, shares the Republicans' desire for a "strong State" and their demand that its form be indivisible. He accepts the principle advanced by Hobbes that the State is in harmony with its own purpose when, by concentrating all its power, it is thus able to ensure both its own security and that of the individual citizen. But he explicitly rejects the distinction between "natural right" and "civil right" (cf. *The Letters*, L, to Jelles, and note XXXIII to the *TTP*), along with the concepts of the "social contract" and "representation". Moreover, not only does he believe that democracy too can be "absolute", but he proposes – in opposition to all of his contemporaries – that the "absolutely absolute" State (*omnino absolutum*) would, given certain conditions, be a democracy (*TP*, VIII, 3; VIII, 7; XI, 1). But, at the same time, this reasoning leads him to the question of why the "free Republic" of the *grands bourgeois* of Amsterdam and The Hague *was not* absolute in this sense, and doubtless never could have been. This in turn leads him to a question that neither Hobbes nor Machiavelli ever asked themselves, and which the *TTP* had only treated from one angle: that of the basis of State power in the people, that is, in movements originating from within the "multitude" itself. This was an entirely new question for the period, at least as an object of theoretical analysis. One might even say that this question forced Spinoza to prove himself more of a "politician" than the "politicians" themselves.

The Plan of the *Tractatus Politicus*

In the *first section* (chapters I–V), Spinoza describes the methods of political science, defines its fundamental notions (right, State, sovereignty, civil freedom) and poses the *general problem*, that of the "preservation" of political regimes. In the *second section* (from chapter VI onwards), he examines the ways in which this problem can be resolved for each of the three types of regime: *monarchy, aristocracy* and *democracy*.

Since the work was not completed, the argument is left hanging just at the crucial moment. In certain conditions, both monarchy and aristocracy may be "absolute". But what of democracy? This gap in his theory was apparently accidental, but it still continues to disturb Spinoza's commentators, who are often tempted to use their imaginations to try and supply the missing steps. But is this possible? Our answer to this question will depend on how we understand the order in which the argument is presented, for this order is open to several different interpretations.

If we consider the notions with which Spinoza begins as "first truths" (or even "first causes"), then all that remains to be done is to work out the detail of their application. In that case, Spinoza's failure to complete his work would be relatively unimportant, since all the essential information is already there. With the help of certain proleptic passages, it will then be possible to reconstruct the theory of the democratic regime, which from the outset has been presented to us as "the best" of the three types of government.

Perhaps it was Spinoza's intention to proceed in this manner, that is, deductively. However, when one tries to come to terms with the text of the *TP*, it rapidly becomes apparent that this is not quite how it worked in practice. The *TP*, like the *TTP*, is a quest, whose successful outcome cannot be guaranteed a priori. Doubtless the author has to have a few general notions that can be taken as given at the start. But, for Spinoza, general notions are not the same as effective knowledge, which can only be a knowledge of singular realities. We can push this argument to its limit: only a historical State is a singular reality, and the categorisation of regimes into types is merely a theoretical tool for analysing this singularity. Our principle of interpretation, then, must be reversed: *general notions do not resolve anything, they simply serve to pose a problem*. To define right as "power" is immediately to discover all the difficulties and contradictions that lie concealed within the fundamental question of the preservation of the State. By examining how this question arises in relation to different regimes, one can gradually determine the conditions of its solution. Whence another question which we should bear in mind: in the passage from monarchy to aristocracy, and thence to a hypothetical democracy, are we moving any nearer to that solution? There is one obvious thread which runs through the stages of this process: the less sovereignty is physically identified with one fraction of society (in the limiting case, with one individual), the more it will tend to coincide with the people as a whole, and the stronger and more stable it will be.

But at the same time, the more difficult it will be to imagine its unity (its *unanimity*) and its indivisibility (its capacity for *decision*), and the more complicated it will be to organise them in practice (cf. *TP*, VI, 4).

But there is another, less direct, logic that can also be seen at work in the text. The traditional classification of "regimes" into different "types" may simply serve to allow Spinoza to isolate different aspects of the problem of absolute sovereignty and to work out their implications. In that case, we would be dealing with a dynamic set of "models", situated somewhere between an abstract idea of the State and the complexity of real politics. Each model would then constitute a further step towards a global realism, but their sequence would not in any way form a straightforward progression. Thus the analysis of monarchy, which forces Spinoza to confront the problems posed by the inheritance of the royal function and the privileges of the nobility, focuses on the latent contradiction between two types of social solidarity: that based on kinship and that based on right (or on citizenship). The first form of aristocracy (considered in chapter VIII) foregrounds the question of the struggle or inequality of class between patricians and plebeians. By going on to introduce a second form of "federal" aristocracy in chapter IX, created by the alliance of several relatively autonomous municipalities, Spinoza is able to "overdetermine" the problem of class by introducing another contradiction: that between centralisation and provincialism. In this way, he poses the question of the relationship between the unity of power and the unity of national territory and population. What further problem would then be raised by the analysis of democracy? We can propose as a hypothesis that it would force us to examine, in its most general terms, the question of the passions of the multitude. These passions are an obstacle to rational decision making in the operation of any kind of assembly, since "each man strives to make the others live in conformity with his own nature [*ingenium*], approve what he approves, and reject what he rejects" (*TP*, I, 5). This is what the *Ethics* defines as *ambition*. Thus behind the question which arises for any regime – is the multitude governable? – lies another, which conditions to varying degrees this first question: to what extent is the multitude capable of governing its own passions?

Right and Power

In the *TTP*, Spinoza had defined the notion of "right" in the form of a thesis — "the right of the individual is co-extensive with its determinate power" (*TTP*, 237). In the *TP*, he goes on to develop all the consequences of this definition and, in the process, to demonstrate his originality as a theorist. Taken literally, this thesis means that the notion of "right" has no *priority*, for that priority belongs to the notion of "power". One might say that the word *right* (*Jus*) is used to express the originary reality of power (*potentia*) in the language of politics. But by doing so we have not introduced a separation between right and power, since the word *originary* does not imply *proceeding from* or *grounded in* (which is why, in particular, any interpretation of Spinoza's definition as a variant on the idea of "might is right" is clearly mistaken). Spinoza's purpose here is not to justify the notion of right, but to form an adequate idea of its determinations, of the way in which it works. In this sense, his formula can be glossed as meaning that *the individual's right includes all that he is effectively able to do and to think in a given set of conditions*:

> Now from the fact that the power of things in nature to exist and act is really the power of God, we can easily see what the right of nature is. For since God has the right to do everything, and God's right is simply God's power conceived as completely free, it follows that each thing in nature has as much right from nature as it has power to exist and act; since the power by which it exists and acts is nothing but the completely free power of God.
>
> By the right of nature, then, I mean the actual laws or rules of nature in accordance with which all things come to be; that is, the actual power of nature. Thus the natural right of nature as a whole, and consequently the natural right of each individual, extends as far as its power. Hence everything a man does in accordance with the laws of his nature, he does by the sovereign right of nature, and he has as much right against other things in nature as he has power and strength. (*TP*, II, 3–4)

We should understand by this that the right of each man is always *one part* of the power of nature as a whole: as such, it enables him to act on all the other parts. Consequently, right is measured by the same scale as *individuality*; for nature is not an undifferentiated whole. On the contrary, it is a complex made up of distinct individuals who themselves are each more or less autonomous, and more or less complex. We should understand too that the notion of right corresponds only to an *actual reality*, and therefore to an *activity*. Thus a formula such as "men are born and remain free and equal in their rights" would have no sense from this perspective. The fact is that, in practice, men are of unequal strength, unless some balance of power (that is, some kind of State) is instituted in order to equalise relations between them. As for birth, it certainly does not mark the moment at which the individual is first able to affirm his right. On the contrary, it is the moment at which the individual is, in himself, most powerless. It is through the protection of others that he is first able to acquire his right. In general, the idea of a "theoretical" right, which is conceived as a *capacity* to act and which may either be recognised and exercised or not, is an absurdity or a mystification. It is an inadequate way of indicating either one's hope of increasing one's power, or one's regret for a former power that has since been supplanted by the power of another.

In this way, two of the classic conceptions of right are eliminated:

- on the one hand, that which relates individual and collective rights to the prior existence of a *given judicial order* (a system of institutions or a recognised authority such as, for instance, divine justice), that is to say, an "objective" conception in which a right *authorises* certain actions, certain acts of possession, and forbids others;
- on the other, that which construes a right as being the manifestation of the *free will* of the human individual as opposed to "things" (or everything that may be classified as a "thing"), that is to say, a "subjective" conception, in which right is the expression of a universal human characteristic, which contains a *demand* for recognition. As we shall see, Spinoza explicitly criticises this point of view (*TP*, II, 7).

The first consequence of this double exclusion is that the notion of right is *not* defined, at the outset, in relation to the notion of *duty*. Like the power it expresses, a right does not initially have an "opposite" or a "corresponding element". But it does necessarily have certain de facto limits, for an unlimited right would be the expression of an unlimited power – a notion that can only make sense in relation to God or to nature as a whole. The abstract idea of rights and duties that might be defined once and for all time is therefore replaced by another pair of correlative notions, which contrast the fact of *independence*, the individual's ability to determine his actions without constraint, to "have possession of his own right" (*sur juris esse*), with the fact of his *dependence* on the right of one or several other individuals (that is, on their power) (*esse alterius juris, sub alterius potestate*) (*TP*, II, 9ff.). This is the fundamental relation.

This opposition does not, however, constitute an absolute antithesis. As we have seen, only God (that is, nature as a whole, the sum of all natural powers) is absolutely independent (since he contains within himself all individualities and all alterities). In practice, when dealing with particular finite natural entities, all of which are reciprocally interdependent, there is a combination of dependence and independence. In particular, every man affirms his individuality against other men (and against other non-human individuals: animals, physical forces, and so on), and at the very same time is more or less completely dependent on them. If each man's right is the expression of his power, then it necessarily includes these two aspects. It is, by definition, a category which refers to relations of force – relations which can vary and which will necessarily evolve.

However, we should be careful not to interpret this definition simply in terms of conflict. Of course conflicts exist, and what Spinoza calls the "state of nature" is a limiting case in which individual powers would in practice always be incompatible with one another. In such a situation, each individual would find himself in a state of total dependency, without that dependency contributing in any way to his independence. Individuality itself would then be at risk. Such a "natural" state is by its very nature unviable, not to say unimaginable – save in times of historical catastrophe, when society disintegrates, or in cases, which may simply be metaphors, such as tyrannical regimes, where individuals are terrorised to the point that their lives are reduced to a level that is less than "human". To be in the power of others, to depend upon their power, can also constitute a positive condition through which one can, up to a point, preserve and affirm one's own individuality. The question then arises as to how one may know on what level a

balance can be achieved: to what extent will the rights of the
different individuals involved add up, or, even better, multiply,
and to what extent will they neutralise each other, or even lead to
a cycle of mutual destruction?

It is precisely on this basis that we can analyse the interrelationship of the different "rights" in the construction of a judicial system
– as a system of power. Those rights are compatible which express
powers that can be added or multiplied together; those rights are
incompatible which correspond to powers that will mutually
destroy one another.

From this equivalence between rights and powers, Spinoza
immediately deduces a series of critical consequences that will play
a key role in any political analysis:

• *Equality of rights* itself constitutes a right or a power, which may
  or may not exist, according to the circumstances; it supposes
  certain conditions. Spinoza explicitly points this out in relation
  to the problem of a federal State (*TP*, IX, 4). In an anarchic
  situation, close to the "state of nature", the equality of individuals exists "in imagination rather than in fact", as does their
  independence (*TP*, II, 15). True equality, as opposed to this
  empty equality, between certain men, or between all the citizens
  of a State, can only exist as the joint result of institutions
  combined with a collective praxis. It will only emerge if
  everyone recognises it as being in their interest.

• *Contractual relations* between individuals (by which they undertake reciprocal commitments to exchange goods and render
  services) are not the consequence of a prior obligation but the
  constitution of a new right, or a new power, whose nature is
  "double". Only a superior power (for example, a sovereign who
  chooses to enforce respect for commitments entered into by a
  law of the State) can, therefore, prevent contracts from being
  broken when the interests which led them to be signed no
  longer exist (*TP*, II, 12–13). But if this power sought to enforce
  such a law in a great many simultaneous cases it would thereby
  put its own power at risk. The same is true of contracts made
  between States, save that in this case there is no superior
  authority, and the decisive factor is therefore the interests of the
  parties involved (*TP*, III, 11ff.).

- The principle of the *equivalence of right and de facto power*, which is so shocking to intuitive morality, is therefore, when seen in relation to the problem of the balance of power, only a consequence and not a constitutive principle. In particular, as was already explained in the *TTP*, the sovereign's right never extends any further than his capacity to enforce effective obedience (by whatever means that capacity is determined, taking into account the convictions of his subjects). The sanctions which the sovereign imposes upon delinquents, criminals and rebels do not express the need to make them respect some higher "prohibition", but simply the need to ensure his own preservation. Such sanctions can be called rational to the extent that reason prescribes that the preservation of the State is preferable to its dissolution.

- But then how does the distinction between passion and reason affect the definition of right? According to the same rule: *there are rights of passion and rights of reason*. Both kinds of right express a natural power. Yet these two kinds of right are not symmetrical: if passion excludes and destroys reason, reason does not in itself imply the destruction of every passion – it is merely a superior power which dominates the passions. This problem is closely related to that of dependence/independence: Spinoza calls the right of the individual for whom reason is stronger than passion and whose independence is greater than his dependency, freedom. Is one superiority the cause of the other? To be able to say this, we would first need to establish not only that the passions create forms of dependency in relation to others (which experience suggests is true), but that reason can make us independent (which is less obviously the case). Yet all other things being equal, it seems likely that the most rational individuals will also be those who are the least dependent upon the passions of others (*TP*, II, 5; II, 7–8). This leads us back to the problem of the difference between "independence" and isolation or solitude, that is, to the material conduct of life in civil societies. Reason counsels us to seek peace and security by pooling our individual powers, and this will in turn bestow upon us the greatest possible degree of real independence.

The "Body Politic"

Spinoza's constant theme in the *TP* is that politics is the science (both theoretical and applied) of the preservation of the State. Politics, therefore, has a purpose (which obviously does not authorise it to resort to arguments in terms of *finality* – such arguments might be considered the form of "superstition" that is proper to it). From the point of view of the State itself, this purpose takes the form of a higher imperative: "the common welfare" and "public order" (peace, security, obedience to the law). One might also say that politics tends to preserve both the "matter" of the State and the "form" of its institutions (and thus, the right/power of its sovereign, whether that be a king, an aristocracy or the people). But as the "matter" of the State is nothing other than a certain system of stable relationships coordinating the movements of individuals (*facies civitatis*) (*TP*, VI, 2), these two formulae correspond to a single reality: the preservation of the *individuality* of the State itself.

The State must therefore be imagined as an individual or, more exactly, as an *individual of individuals*, having a "body" and a "soul" or mind (*mens*) (*TP*, III, 1–2; III, 5; IV, 2; VI, 19; VIII, 19; IX, 14; X, 1). "[I]n the political order the whole body of citizens must be thought of as equivalent to an individual in the state of nature" (*TP*, VII, 22; translation modified). This would seem to place Spinoza squarely in the line of Hobbes (the *Leviathan*) and, more generally, of a whole tradition which defines the State as an individual and which runs from the ancient Greeks to the present day. However, we must press this point further, since such an assimilation covers in reality a wide range of different views. The individuality of the State may be thought of as either metaphorical or real, as "natural" or "artificial", as a mechanistic or an organic solidarity, as a self-organising principle of the State or an effect of its supernatural finality. Therefore, everything will depend upon the content Spinoza himself gives to this definition.

The preservation of the human individual and of the individual State both depend upon the application of one and the same causal principle:

> Anything in nature can be conceived adequately whether it is actually
> in being or not. Thus neither its coming into being nor its persistence

in being can be deduced from its definition; for its essence in thought is the same after it has come into being as it was before it existed. Its persistence in being, then, cannot follow from its essence any more than its coming into being can; it needs the same power to continue in being as it needs to come into being. It follows that the power by which things in nature exist, and by which, in consequence, they act, can be none other than *the eternal power of God*. For suppose it were some other power, created by God; then, not being able to preserve itself, it would not be able to preserve things in nature either, but would itself need the same power to persist in being as it needed to be created. (*TP*, II, 2)

This principle of *continuous production* applies equally to human individuals (for whom Spinoza prefers to use the indefinite term *unusquisque*, "each and every one") (*TP*, II, 5–8; III, 18) and to the body politic (*TP*, III, 12). In each case, existence is considered not only as a form of natural production but as a process of reproduction for the elements of the individual and the power that binds them together, which enables them to stand up to the action of external forces ("luck"). This defines an internal necessity but does not thereby abolish the effect of the "laws of nature as a whole". Spinoza expresses this thought by a phrase which occupies a strategic position in his work: neither the human individual nor the State itself is in nature as "a State within a State" (*imperium in imperio*). Neither possesses an absolute autonomy.

However, there is a considerable difference of degree between the power of the isolated human individual and the power of the "individual of individuals" that is the State. Indeed, it is enough for there to be a qualitative difference between the two. Isolated individuals are, in practice, incapable of guaranteeing their own preservation over a long period of time. The State, on the other hand, can, if it is well constructed, endure through its own strength (*TP*, III, 11). Measured by the scale of an individual life, the life of the State may well come to resemble "a sort of eternity". At this point, the analogy between the two gives way to a reciprocity, which also constitutes a much more concrete relationship: in order to preserve their own lives, individuals need each other; thus they must be led, by the pursuit of their own interests, to will the preservation of the State (*TP*, VII, 4; VII, 22; VIII, 24; VIII, 31; X, 6). In return, in order to preserve itself the State must seek to preserve the lives of the individuals, by guaranteeing them the security that is the fundamental condition of civic obedience. In a State that has succumbed to anarchy or has been subjugated by the power of its enemies, loyalty to the State disappears (*TP*, X, 9–10; chapter IV). The "best regime" is therefore, by definition, that which achieves the strongest correlation between the security of the individual and the stability of its institutions:

> The best condition [*status*] of a commonwealth [*imperium*] is easily discovered from the purpose of political order: which is simply peace and security of life. Accordingly, the best commonwealth is one in which men live in harmony, and the laws are kept unbroken. Rebellions, wars, and contemptuous disregard for law must certainly be attributed to the corrupt condition of the commonwealth rather than to the wickedness of its subjects. For citizens [*civiles*] are not born, but made. Besides, men's natural passions are the same everywhere; hence if wickedness is more dominant and crime more prevalent in one commonwealth than in another, this is certainly due to the fact that the first has not done enough to promote harmony, has not framed its laws with sufficient foresight, and so has failed to acquire its absolute right as a commonwealth. For a political order which has not removed the causes of civil strife, where war is a constant threat, and the laws are often broken, differs little from a veritable state of nature, where everyone lives according to his temperament [*ingenium*] with great danger to his life. (*TP*, V, 2)

If this correlation were total, that is, if the form of the State were no more of a "threat" to the security of the individual than the activity of the individual were a danger for the institutions of the State, then the result would be a perfect body politic, which could be described as free or rational (*TP*, V, 6; VIII, 7). But in one sense, if that were the case, there would be no more history, and no more politics.

Up to this point, Spinoza has done no more than work systematically through lines of argument that had already been sketched out in the *TTP*. In other words, he has done no more than spell out the consequences of a strictly immanent conception of historical causality in which the only factors that intervene are individual powers, composite powers founded on individual powers and the *reciprocal action* of these two types of power.[3] But,

[3] The term is used in a letter to Oldenburg (*The Letters*, XXXII) and reflects the

as we pointed out earlier, what was given as a solution in the *TTP* is now taken to constitute a problem. What is the mode of reciprocal action that characterises the existence of a body politic? This needs to be defined in more concrete terms. In order to do so, we shall now look at Spinoza's analysis of the causes that lead to the dissolution of the different types of regime.

Some of these causes are stated in terms that are specific to a given type of State. Others are general causes, and only their forms will vary according to the structures of the given institutions. There are also *external* causes, the most important of which is war. All societies are threatened by war, because States relate to one another in the same way as do individuals in the state of nature (*TP*, III, 11; VII, 7). The stronger the State is internally, the better it will be able to defend itself. But, at the same time, all the motives that cause a State to prefer war to peace (the existence of a military caste, the sovereign's ambition and desire for glory, the temptation to export internal conflicts or to neutralise them by a war of conquest) are indirectly causes of the State's destruction. Leaving to one side the irreducible role played by "luck" or "destiny", the true causes of dissolution are therefore always *internal*.

These internal causes are not all equally serious. The least important are those that result from *disrespect for the law* on the part of individuals, which can vary on a scale from outright disobedience to simply attempting to interpret the decisions of the sovereign so as to suit oneself (*TP*, III, 3–4). The mere fact that a citizen or group of citizens claims to know better than the State itself what is needed to protect the general public contains the seed of the State's dissolution (*TP*, III, 10; IV, 2). Paralleling this phenomenon is the *arbitrary use of power*, through which authority degenerates into tyranny. This may happen when a monarch has pretensions to wield a power that exceeds his real strength (*TP*, VI, 5) or when an aristocratic patrician class turns into a hereditary caste (*TP*, VIII, 14). It may also take the form of an attempt to impose on the people a kind of government that is in contradiction with their historical traditions (*TP*, VII, 26; IX, 14). In every case, a certain

conclusions of the arguments that can be found in the *Ethics* on the conservation of the individual's form: cf. *Ethics*, IIP9 and the brief account of the nature of bodies that follows at P13.

impotence seeks compensation in terror and corruption (*TP*, VII, 13, 21; VIII, 29), which in the end only aggravates its initial weakness. The mere exercise of power itself is then perceived by the individual as a threat to his existence or dignity (*TP*, IV, 4). When the State has grown so "mad" that it threatens to deprive its citizens of the minimum viable measure of individuality, below which they will effectively be dead to themselves, it always in the end provokes the *outrage of the multitude*, and this outrage destroys it (*TP* III, 9; VII, 2; X, 8; and the whole of chapter IV).

In the final analysis, whether the violence of individuals provokes the violence of the State or individuals find they can no longer resist the violence of the authorities, save by violence (*TP*, VII, 30), we are led to the same conclusion: no body politic can exist without being subject to the latent threat of civil war ("sedition"), whether between different factions of the ruling class or between the rulers and the ruled. This is the cause of causes, which ultimately determines the efficacy of every other cause. Whence this fundamental thesis: *its own citizens (cives) are always a greater threat to the body politic than any external enemies (hostes)* (*TP*, VI, 6). Every type of regime discovers the truth of this rule through its own experience. In a monarchy, sedition can stem from the existence of a hereditary aristocracy (*TP*, VII, 10), the resort to mercenary armies (*TP*, VII, 12) and dynastic rivalry (*TP*, VI, 37). In an aristocracy, it can stem from inequalities within the patrician class (*TP*, VIII, 11), the corruption of civil servants (*TP*, VIII, 29), rivalry between cities (*TP*, IX, 3; IX, 9), ·the ambition of military leaders, encouraged in times of crisis by the people's desire for a saviour (*TP*, VIII, 9; X, 1), and finally (and most frequently) the class struggle between patricians and plebeians, who are effectively treated as foreigners within the city (*TP*, VIII, 1–2, 11, 13–14, 19, 41, 44; X, 3).

How should we interpret these analyses? To begin with, they extend the dialectic of the institutions of the State that was sketched out in the *TTP*, introducing variants according to the different types of regime. They demonstrate the futility of denouncing the "vices" of human nature (or of a specific group of men) since the fundamental cause of the citizens' "vices" (as of their virtues) always lies in the actions of institutions (*TP*, III, 3; V, 2–3; VII, 7; VII, 12; IX, 14; X, 1–4). From this we may conclude that the key to the protection of the body politic lies in the quality of its institutions. But, in the course of these analyses, something new has also emerged, which modifies the meaning of this conclusion. When taken together, the causes of the dissolution of the body politic form a cycle. This cycle is entirely immanent to the natural constitution of the State, that is, it expresses a certain (contradictory) relationship between its constituent powers (*TP*, II, 18; IV, 4). Or, to put it another way, nature is effectively identical with history. More than that, the multitude as such, not only in its quantitative sense (the "majority" of citizens) but also in its qualitative sense (the collective behaviour of individuals who are brought together en masse), has become the decisive concept in this analysis of the State. Thus the political problem no longer has two terms but three. "Individual" and "State" are in fact abstractions, which only have meaning in relation to one another. In the final analysis, each of them serves merely to express one modality through which the *power of the multitude* can be realised as such.

This argument, then, brings us back to the idea of balance, of "self-limitation". As we have already seen, the State that is "strong", that is "absolute", is the State that has its own power under control. The least "absolute" of all States is that which has to legislate against those vices which it has itself produced (*TP*, X, 4–6). But the balance that characterises the strong State is now seen always already to contain within itself the idea of an antagonism. For the strength of the multitude is a power for discord as well as a power for harmony, and it is in relation to the "passions" of the multitude that the problem of balance or moderation arises. The solution to this problem will require a relative "neutralisation" of this antagonism. A simple resolution at the level of "government" is no longer imaginable, for there is no external point from which the multitude can be governed, not even in the form in which Hobbes had imagined it. In a superb passage, Spinoza explains how the degeneration of the institutions of the State corrupts both the "masters" (those who rule) and their subjects (those who are ruled):

> Those who confine to the common people the vices which exist in all human beings will perhaps greet my contentions with ridicule, on the ground that "there is no moderation in the masses, they terrorise unless

they are afraid", that "the common people is either an obsequious
servant or a domineering master", that "it has no truth or judgement
in it", and so on. But all men have one and the same nature: it is
power and culture which mislead us. Hence "when two men do the
same thing we often say that the one may do it with impunity but not
the other; not because the thing, but because the person who does it,
is different". Pride is characteristic of rulers. If men are puffed up by
appointment for a year, what can we expect of nobles who hold office
without end? But their arrogance is adorned with refinement, magnifi-
cence, lavishness, with an harmonious blend of vices, a sophisticated
folly, and an elegant depravity; so that the faults which when viewed
singly and in isolation are base and ugly, because then most obvious,
seem honourable and becoming to the ignorant and inexperienced.
Again, "there is no moderation in the masses, they terrorise unless they
are afraid" because freedom and slavery are not easily combined.
Finally, that "there is no truth or judgement in the common people"
is not surprising, when they are kept in ignorance of the main affairs of
state, and merely guess at the facts from the little that cannot be
concealed. For to suspend judgement is a rare virtue. Thus to keep all
the work of government a secret from the citizens, and then to expect
them not to misjudge it and put the worst construction on everything,
is the height of folly. For if the common people could practise self-
restraint, and suspend judgement when the evidence is insufficient, or
could make correct judgements about public affairs with little information to go on, they would certainly be more worthy to rule than to
be ruled. However, as I said, all men have the same nature. (*TP*, VII,
27)[4]

We can summarise the argument here in the following terms:
rulers and ruled, sovereign and citizens, all belong to the multitude. And
the fundamental question is always, in the final analysis, whether
the multitude is able to govern itself, that is, whether it can increase
its own power. In concrete terms, this has two consequences:

1. Democracy is an inherently problematic concept, since it
corresponds to the mode of existence of a multitude that has
already found its own internal balance, that is already substantially
"unanimous".

2. The balance that is required is not a stasis, like the

---

[4] The first four quotations are from Tacitus, *Annals*, I, xxix, 3; Livy XXIV, XXV, 8;
Tacitus, *Histories*, I, xxxii, 1; and Terence, *Adelphi*, 823–5, respectively.

arrangement of organs in a body or the order of a judicial system; it emerges when individuals work together on a common project. In other words, the "soul" of the body politic is not a representation but a praxis. The central question then is, how does the State decide?

Decision: The Soul of the State

Individuals rarely "decide", in the strong sense of the term. What they mistake for their will is most often only ignorance of the passions which lead them to prefer certain actions to others. Even the minimal rationality provided by an awareness of their own interest is not enough to protect them from fantasies of impotence or omnipotence, from fatalism or from superstition. As for the multitude, it is a contradictory power, internally divided against itself: as such, it is unable to decide anything. It lacks the minimum of coherence that would allow it to correct its errors, to adjust ends to means. In most societies, moreover, it is denied both rights and access to information. It is simply a medium in which different passions resonate with one another, in which the "fluctuations" of the city's soul are amplified, often to extremes. Yet, if a unified will is to emerge at the level of the State, the multitude must be involved in its production. How in concrete terms might this be possible?

Let us begin by considering monarchy. The first question that arises is, who, in reality, decides? It might seem to be the king himself. But, even leaving to one side those frequent cases in which the king is a weak individual, either in body or in mind, the fact is that a single individual is quite incapable of bearing the full burden of the State (*TP*, VI, 5). He needs counsellors to keep him informed, friends or relatives to protect him, assistants to communicate his orders and see that they are carried out. So, in fact, it is these people who decide. "Absolute" monarchies are thus concealed aristocracies, where real power is in the hands of a caste. This caste, made up of courtiers and nobles, is inevitably divided by rivalry and ambition. When a single man is at the head of the State, replacing him is the simplest operation imaginable (*TP*, VII, 14, 23). The temptation might even be considered natural, given that the king is mortal and that at each moment of succession there is the risk that sovereignty will "revert to the people" (*TP*, VII, 25). To protect himself from his rivals and to ensure his control over his own succession, the king, who is theoretically all-powerful, is thus obliged to encourage rivalry between different groups. This he does by granting privileges to certain favourites and by "plotting against his subjects" (*TP*, V, 7; VI, 6; VII, 29; translation modified). And in this way, he gradually paralyses his own ability to act.

In order for a monarchy to achieve all the power of which it is capable, there is only one rational strategy. All traces of corporatism must be eliminated, and the decision-making process must be grounded in the masses. At the same time, steps must be taken to ensure that the unity of the final decision cannot be challenged. Draconian laws are therefore necessary to govern the operation of the councils that are responsible for gathering and focusing different political "options" towards the monarch (*TP*, VI, 25; VII, 5). We should notice that the mechanisms Spinoza describes are not only *representative* but also as *egalitarian* as possible. The king must play no role in the process of deliberation and elaboration of policy. A fortiori, there must be no "State secrets" to which only he has access (*TP*, VII, 29). He is not a "leader" who in himself could guarantee the security of the State. Yet his role is not in any way superfluous, for there is a difference between deliberation and decision. Even sanctioning a majority opinion is a substantive action. Without this central function, such a system would be incapable of producing concrete results but would waver endlessly between the different majorities that would constantly be dissolving and reforming. Because the different moments of the decision-making process, and the responsibility for supervising its execution, are divided between an assembly and the monarch, the system is saved from a radical uncertainty, and the impulses of the multitude are stabilised. Or rather, the multitude is thus able to create its own stability, by "electing" from within itself (through some kind of formal mechanism) an individual who has responsibility for drawing debate to a conclusion. In this way, we might say that the king is the only individual in the body politic who has no "opinion" of his own, *no interiority*. In himself, he does not "think" any differently than the multitude. But without him the multitude would be incapable of thinking clearly and distinctly and so would be unable to save itself. In this, and only in this sense, it is strictly true to say that the King is "the mind of the city" (*TP*, VI, 18–19; translation modified).

What then of aristocracy? In some respects, the situation is simply reversed. An aristocracy cannot be transformed into an egalitarian regime without collapsing, for it is precisely the domination of a given class that is to be preserved as such. It is therefore necessary that the "plebeians" should be totally excluded from both the process of deliberation and the final moment of decision. From a political perspective, all those subjects who are not citizens are foreigners to the State (*TP*, VIII, 9). The decisions of the patrician class must therefore be taken by secret ballot, so as to prevent people from contesting them and in order to discourage clientelism and the formation of pressure groups (*TP*, VIII, 27). On the other hand, the patrician assemblies must not be deprived of their specifically patrician character. On the contrary, the aim is to ensure that when they pursue their own (class) interest, they are thereby pursuing the general interest too (*TP*, X, 6–8). This convergence of interests is possible because an assembly, unlike a monarch, is "eternal": as its members age, grow ill or die, they are replaced by new arrivals (*TP*, VIII, 3; X, 2).

Such a system, however, still needs to be grounded in the masses. Whence this fundamental rule: *in order for an aristocracy to be viable, it must enlarge the number of its members as far as possible* (*TP*, VIII, 1–4, 11–13). It must do so in order both to increase its own strength and to reflect "statistically" the whole range of opinions to be found in the masses. The more members the patrician class can boast, the more effectively it will be able to maintain its exclusive right of decision and thus its hold on power (*TP*, VIII, 3, 17, 19, 29, etc.). Such an aristocracy, then, is in fact an open and expansive ruling class (a "bourgeoisie"?). But this rule does not automatically resolve every difficulty. How is one to prevent a body politic that has several heads from ending up effectively "headless" (*TP*, IX, 14; translation modified)? Electing a president is either a mere artifice or a change of regime (*TP*, VIII, 17–18). The true solution to this problem lies in the application of the principle of pure majority rule, and all the different (and complex) constitutional arrangements which Spinoza proposes are intended to enact this principle and ensure that it is properly applied (*TP*, VIII, 35ff.).

While it may be "representative", the principle of majority rule in its pure form excludes the possibility of forming permanent political parties. Here Spinoza seems to be pursuing two different ideas at once: the idea that the assemblies of collective governments can elaborate rational choices through discussion; and the idea that if every opinion is given some say in the process of arriving at a decision, then the result has the best possible chance of corresponding to the general interest and thus of being acceptable to all. If that is true, then the formation of parties, which would substantially reduce the number of opinions in play, would therefore be a cause of systematic error.

One last remark is necessary: it does not follow that because a decision is rational, it will therefore automatically be respected. Spinoza here introduces one final mechanism, which corresponds implicitly to the distinction between two different sorts of apparatus: that of the *government* and that of the *administration*. The plebeians should be excluded from the decision-making bodies, but they should provide the state with its bureaucrats (*TP*, VIII, 17; VIII, 44). In this way the different classes, though unequal in respect of sovereignty, will both be involved in the running of the State and can both identify the State with their own interest. Thus the majority principle can be a means of producing unanimity. Not only will the ruling assembly be governed "as if by a single mind" (*TP*, VIII, 19; translation modified), but this mind will direct the body politic as a whole, *as if* the multitude were one single individual.

The decision-making mechanisms presented here by Spinoza attempt to satisfy two requirements at the same time. On the one hand, they try to constitute what we would call a "State apparatus" as the true locus of political power. According to their respective modalities, each regime thus tends to identify its "sovereign" with the functional unity of this apparatus. On the other hand, they begin to subject this apparatus to a process of "democratisation". Certainly, there is no clear answer to the question of what institutions and what methods for regulating conflict would be appropriate to a regime that was democratic from the outset. But this aporia is compensated for by the fact that each of the other regimes, as it tends towards its own "perfection", opens the way to democracy. For Spinoza, the institutions whose purpose is to distil a single opinion, and thus a choice, out of the "fluctuation of minds" tend by this very fact to produce a concrete "union" of hearts and minds around a common purpose. But if that is so, then it is imaginable that the multitude might rule itself. And the more such a result is effectively produced, the more the juridical distinction between a "monarchy" or an "aristocracy", on the one hand, and a "democracy", on the other, will prove to be purely formal and abstract. In the limiting case, the only difference left will be the name.

Some of Spinoza's postulates may be surprising, such as the hypothesis of a monarchy independent of any nobiliary caste. But this hypothesis does correspond to a known tendency of classic "absolutist" States. Even more surprisingly, the egalitarianism of Spinoza's monarchy fits well with the hypothesis of a "bourgeois monarch". It also seems to anticipate the "presidential" and "imperial" regimes that were to emerge several centuries later. His model of the aristocratic regime is a somewhat different case. The rational capacity for collective decision making on which it depends can only be saved from being undermined by internal tensions if the ruling class is enlarged until it encompasses the people in its entirety, save only for those who are "natural dependents", that is, women and servants (*TP*, VIII, 14; XI, 3–4). Doubtless this hypothesis presupposes that the wealth of all citizens can grow indefinitely too. But however that may be, one thing is clear: democracy as it is presented in the *TP* is only imaginable on the basis of the dialectic between these two forms of rationalisation of the State, one of which begins by privileging equality, and the other, freedom.

4

The *Ethics*:
A Political Anthropology

We have followed Spinoza through the two stages of his work on political theory and have sought to bring out both the continuity between them and the contrasts. Yet we have hardly begun to resolve the crucial question, that of the reciprocal implication of philosophy and politics. Did Spinoza himself pose this question explicitly? Did he try to explain how these two domains are united? The answer would appear to be yes. In his later work, he went on to elaborate the ideas that had underpinned the arguments of the *TTP* and the *TP* into a full-blown conceptual framework for an anthropology (a theory of "human nature"). In doing so, he gave a directly political significance to the difference between his own philosophy and the theories of all earlier philosophers. In this chapter I will attempt to show how he did this, by examining his treatment of three specific problems: the problem of sociability; the problem of obedience; and the problem of communication. While continuing to draw on the arguments of the two treatises, I shall here be referring mainly to the *Ethics*. Spinoza spent fifteen years of his life on the system of the *Ethics*, reworking it continuously. His friends and enemies lived in constant expectation of its appearance and were incessantly projecting their own interpretations of what Spinoza *would* say onto its continuing absence. The text was finally published in 1677, shortly after his death.

Sociability

"Nature", "human nature" and "sociability" have always been treated by philosophers as three aspects of a single problem. Does there exist such a thing as a "natural society", defined as such either by its organisation or by its function? If not, does the institution of societies and States "disturb the order of nature", as Spinoza would put it? Our answer to this question will depend upon the way in which we define that "order" (as a cosmic harmony? or as a causal process?) and on the antitheses we set up in opposition to it (violence, artifice or some *other order*, which might be, for example, juridical or spiritual). In general, the way in which a philosophical system construes the concept of nature is simply a way of anticipating, at a distance, the ways in which it will determine the concepts of human individuality and community. But that is not all. The thesis that there exists a natural sociability has been defended by many different authorities: by Aristotle ("Man is by nature *a being who lives for the city*", a phrase later translated by the scholastics as "a sociable animal"), by Bossuet ("Society may be considered as one large family") and by Marx ("In its reality, the essence of humanity is the whole system of its social relationships"). But the meaning of this thesis has changed quite considerably over time and has been made to serve very different political ends.

The same is true of the diametrically opposite thesis, which holds that *society is instituted after*, if not *against*, the spontaneous impulse of nature. Some interpret this as meaning that nature contains a disposition towards life in society that cannot be realised within nature itself (thus, for Rousseau, the man of nature has a "social feeling" for his neighbour, namely pity). For others, nature contains the moral destination of the human community, but the way to that destination through nature is obstructed by the passions (thus Kant, for instance). For others again, even human nature is essentially "egotistical" and anti-social (as for Hobbes, for whom the natural condition of men is the "war of each against all"). Yet while the meaning and the function of these theses may change radically from one context to the next, the *antithetical form itself* has remained constant from ancient Greece to modern Europe. Perhaps then we should look for a meaning in the antithetical form itself, whose duality may serve to mask a single unavoidable fact. And if such a fact exists, is it a reality or a thought? What is there that is *common* to the two ideas of sociability – the natural and the institutional – beyond any differences of anthropological orientation? Perhaps it is the assumption that sociability is a bond which "unites" men, expressing their reciprocal need or their "friendship" (what was known to the Greeks as *philia*, to Christians and to classical Europe as "peace" or "concord"), and that society is the order through which they live out this bond made good.

But Spinoza's thinking disrupts these classical categories and opens up instead a new approach. For him, the alternative between "nature" and "institution" is no longer binding: the problem of social relationships has to be addressed in other terms. But our historical culture, which trains us to see this alternative as ineluctable, can make it difficult for us to *read* Spinoza's theses on sociability. To see where the difficulties lie, let us examine the formulations used in one of the central texts on this question: proposition 37 of part IV of the *Ethics*, together with its two demonstrations and its two scholia.[1]

> *The good which everyone who seeks virtue wants for himself, he also desires for other men; and this desire is greater as his knowledge of God is greater.*
>
> Dem.: Insofar as men live according to the guidance of reason [*ex ductu Rationis*], they are most useful to man (by P35C1); hence (by P19), according to the guidance of reason, we necessarily strive to bring it about that men live according to the guidance of reason. Now, the good which everyone who lives according to the dictate [*dictamen*] of reason (that is, by P24, who seeks virtue) wants for himself is understanding [*intelligere*] (by P26). Therefore, the good which everyone who seeks virtue wants for himself, he also desires for other men.
>
> Next, desire, insofar as it is related to the soul, is the very essence of the soul (by DefAffI). Now the essence of the soul consists in knowledge (by IIP11), which involves knowledge of God (by IIP47). Without this [knowledge the soul] can neither be nor be conceived (by IP15). Hence, as the soul's essence involves a greater knowledge of God, so will the desire also be greater by which one who seeks virtue desires for another the good he wants for himself, QED.
>
> Alternative Dem.: The good which man wants for himself and loves, he will love more constantly if he sees that others love it (by IIIP31). So (by IIIP31C), he will strive to have the others love the same thing. And because this good is common to all (by P36), and all can enjoy it, he will therefore (by the same reason) strive that all may enjoy it. And

---

[1] I have followed Balibar (and Curley) in systematically translating *affectus* as "affect", in order to preserve the distinction between *affectio* (affection) and *passio* (passion). Curley also distinguishes between the two terms *appetitus* (appetite) and *cupiditas* (desire), where Balibar translates both as "desire", on the authority of *Ethics*, IIIP9S. I have followed Balibar's usage of "desire" in his own text, but have not emended Curley's translations on this point. – TRANS.

this striving will be the greater, the more he enjoys this good (by IIIP37), QED.

Schol. 1: He who strives, only because of an affect, that others should love what he loves, and live according to his temperament [*ingenium*], acts only from impulse and is hateful – especially to those to whom other things are pleasing, and who also, therefore, strive eagerly, from the same impulse, to have other men live according to their own temperament. And since the greatest good men seek from an affect is often such that only one can possess it fully, those who love are not of one mind in their love – while they rejoice to sing the praises of the thing they love, they fear to be believed. But he who strives from reason to guide others acts not by impulse, but kindly, generously, and is entirely consistent with himself.

Again, whatever we desire and do of which we are the cause insofar as we have the idea of God, or insofar as we know God, I relate to religion. The desire to do good generated in us by our living according to the guidance of reason, I call piety. The desire by which a man who lives according to the guidance of reason is bound to join others to himself in friendship, I call morality [*Honestas*], and I call that moral which men who live according to the guidance of reason praise; on the other hand, what is contrary to the formation of friendship, I call immoral [*turpe*]. By this, I have also shown what the foundations of the City (*civitas*) are. . . .

Schol. 2: . . . Everyone exists by the sovereign right of Nature, and consequently everyone, by the sovereign right of Nature, does those things which follow from the necessity of his own nature [*suae naturae*]. So everyone, by the sovereign right of Nature, judges what is good and what is evil, considers his own advantage [*utile*] according to his own temperament [*ingenium*] (see P19 and P20), avenges himself (see IIIP40C2), and strives to preserve what he loves and destroy what he hates (see IIIP28). If men lived according to the guidance of reason, everyone would possess this right of his (by P35C1) without any injury to anyone else. But because they are subject to the affects (by P4C), which far surpass man's power, or virtue (by P6), they are often drawn in different directions (by P33) and are contrary to one another (by P34), while they require one another's aid (by P35S).

In order, therefore, that men may be able to live harmoniously and be of assistance to one another, it is necessary for them to give up their natural right and to make one another confident that they will do nothing which could harm others. How it can happen that men who are naturally subject to affects (by P4C), inconstant and changeable (by P33) should be able to make one another confident and have trust in one another, is clear from P7 and IIIP39. No affect can be restrained except by an affect stronger than and contrary to the affect to be restrained, and everyone refrains from doing harm out of timidity regarding a greater harm.

By this law, therefore, society can be maintained, provided it appropriates to itself the right everyone has of avenging himself, and of judging concerning good and evil. In this way society has the power to prescribe a common rule of life [communis vivendi ratio], to make laws, and to maintain them – not by reason, which cannot restrain the affects (by P17S), but by threats. This society, maintained by laws and the power it has of preserving itself, is called a City [civitas], and those who are defended by its law, citizens.

From this we easily understand that there is nothing in the state of nature which, by the agreement of all, is good or evil; for everyone who is in the state of nature considers only his own advantage [utile], and decides what is good and what is evil from his own temperament, and only insofar as he takes account of his own advantage. He is not bound by any law to submit to anyone except himself. So in the state of nature no sin can be conceived.

But in the civil state, of course, it is decided by common agreement what is good or what is evil. And everyone is bound to submit to the City. Sin, therefore, is nothing but disobedience, which for that reason can be punished only by the law of the state. On the other hand, obedience is considered a merit in a citizen, because on that account he is judged worthy of enjoying the advantages of the City.

Again, in the state of nature there is no one who by common consent is Master of anything, nor is there anything in Nature which can be said to be this man's and not that man's. Instead, all things belong to all. So in the state of nature, there cannot be conceived any will to give to each his own, or to take away from someone what is his. That is, in the state of nature nothing is done which can be called just or unjust.

But in the civil state, of course, where it is decided by common consent what belongs to this man, and what to that [things are done which can be called just or unjust]. (translation modified)

A proposition from the *Ethics* cannot be separated from its demonstration. The demonstration determines the meaning of the proposition by showing how it is necessarily connected to other propositions. In this case, however, we have, unusually, *two* demonstrations, which follow completely different lines of argument. If we want to understand, then, what the "foundations of the City" are, it is clear that we must examine how these two demonstrations are both *distinct* from one another and yet express the *same necessity*. The diagram overleaf gives a simplified representation of the logical relations that hold between IVP37 and several groups of prior or complementary propositions.

Let us begin by looking at the first demonstration. On the surface, the reasoning seems to follow a predictable course. Sociability is defined as reciprocity of participation in the greatest good, which is determined by reason. It is through the knowledge of truth (and thus of God, and thus of things) that men are disposed to desire this common Good, and thus their reciprocal usefulness – or in other words, to love one another. So it is not surprising that scholium 1 refers to this "rational" mode of Desire as *Religion* and *Morality*. But this demonstration depends upon two prior propositions. It is here that things begin to get more complicated, thanks to a little word which lies at the heart of the argument: "insofar" (*quatenus*):

IVP35, Dem.: . . . insofar as men live according to the guidance of reason, they are said only to act (by IIIP3). Hence, whatever follows from human nature, insofar as it is defined by reason, must be understood through human nature alone (by IIID2), as through its proximate cause. But because each one, from the laws of his own nature, wants what he judges to be good, and strives to avert what he judges to be evil (by P19), and moreover, because what we judge to be good or evil when we follow the dictate of reason must be good or evil (by IIP41), it follows that insofar as men live according to the guidance of reason, they must do only those things which are good for human nature, and hence, for each man, that is (by P31C), those things which agree with the nature of each man. Hence, insofar as men live according to the guidance of reason, they must always agree among themselves, QED.

Cor. 1: There is no singular thing in Nature which is more useful to man than a man who lives according to the guidance of reason.

For what is most useful to man is what most agrees with his nature (by P31C), that is (as is known through itself), man. But a man acts entirely from the laws of his own nature when he lives according to the guidance of reason (by IIID2), and only *to that extent* must he always agree with the nature of the other man (by P35). . . .

Cor. 2: When each man most seeks what is useful for himself, then men are most useful to one another.

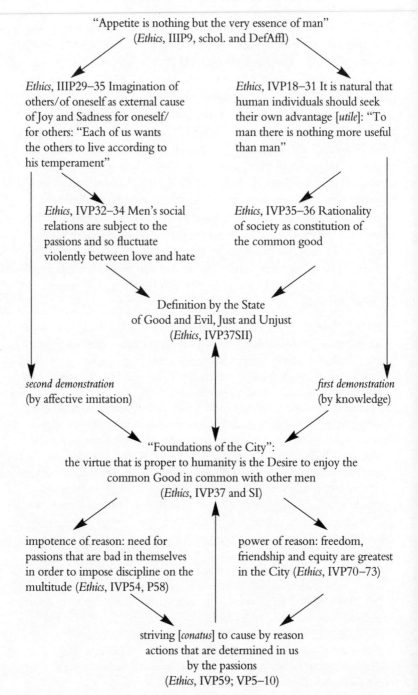

"Appetite is nothing but the very essence of man"
(*Ethics*, IIIP9, schol. and DefAff1)

Ethics, IIIP29–35 Imagination of others/of oneself as external cause of Joy and Sadness for oneself/ for others: "Each of us wants the others to live according to his temperament"

Ethics, IVP18–31 It is natural that human individuals should seek their own advantage [*utile*]: "To man there is nothing more useful than man"

Ethics, IVP32–34 Men's social relations are subject to the passions and so fluctuate violently between love and hate

Ethics, IVP35–36 Rationality of society as constitution of the common good

Definition by the State
of Good and Evil, Just and Unjust
(*Ethics*, IVP37SII)

second demonstration
(by affective imitation)

first demonstration
(by knowledge)

"Foundations of the City":
the virtue that is proper to humanity is the Desire to enjoy the
common Good in common with other men
(*Ethics*, IVP37 and SI)

impotence of reason: need for passions that are bad in themselves in order to impose discipline on the multitude (*Ethics*, IVP54, P58)

power of reason: freedom, friendship and equity are greatest in the City (*Ethics*, IVP70–73)

striving [*conatus*] to cause by reason
actions that are determined in us
by the passions
(*Ethics*, IVP59; VP5–10)

For the more each one seeks what is useful for him, and strives to preserve himself, the more he is endowed with virtue (by P20), or what is the same (by D8), the greater is his power of acting according to the laws of his own nature, that is (by IIIP3), of living from the guidance of reason. . . .

Schol.: What we have just shown is also confirmed by daily experience, which provides so much and such clear evidence that this saying is in almost everyone's mouth: man is a God to man.

Still, it rarely happens that men live according to the guidance of reason. Instead, their lives are so constituted that they are usually envious and burdensome to one another. They can hardly, however, live a solitary life; hence, that definition which makes a man a social animal has been quite pleasing to most. And surely we do derive from the society of our fellow men many more advantages than disadvantages.

So let the satirists laugh as much as they like at human affairs, let the theologians curse them, let melancholics praise as much as they can a life that is uncultivated and wild, let them disdain men and admire the lower animals. Men still find from experience that by helping one another they can provide themselves much more easily with the things they require, and that only by joining forces can they avoid the dangers that threaten on all sides. . . . (translation modified)

The Reason that thus imposes a necessary harmony upon men is not in the least transcendent but simply expresses the power of human nature as it manifests itself and develops in its search for what is useful to each man. It necessarily includes the idea of God, because for men this idea springs directly from their own activity. Yet Reason in itself cannot adequately define human nature. On the contrary, as Spinoza is constantly at pains to point out, human nature is defined both by reason and by ignorance, imagination and passion. Moreover, men live together in accord with the dictates of Reason, to the extent that they completely realise the laws of their own nature. This implies that men will also realise *other laws*, which are equally natural laws. Let us look at the presuppositions that lie behind this passage, by turning to propositions 18 to 31 (part IV). They prepare the present argument by demonstrating that the principle of natural Reason itself (its "dictates") implies a double necessity for each individual: he must both constantly strive [*conatus*] to preserve his own being, and he must seek to constitute, together with other individuals of the same nature as himself, a more powerful individual so as to counterbalance those "external causes [which are] contrary to their nature". In concrete terms, these two necessities are one and the same. Both derive from man's essence, which is his desire to persevere in his being (IIIP6–9). From this, Spinoza concludes that those doctrines which seek to oppose individualism and sociability, as immoral and moral respectively, are simply absurd. But the soundness of his argument depends entirely upon the fact that men are natural individuals, "singular things" of limited power, *just like the infinite number of other individuals that can be found in nature.*

Thus the system of interrelated theses with which we are dealing turns out to be considerably more complex than was at first apparent:

1. Like all natural individuals, men have a direct interest in "agreeing" amongst themselves, insofar as they desire their own preservation.

2. Experience and reason show that this is a necessary truth about society, and the facts confirm it.

3. Reason, in this sense, is part of human nature: it does not have to be "imported" into it from outside.

4. As such, reason cannot claim to define human nature, either exclusively or completely. It does not define it exclusively because human nature is in turn related to a much more general nature, which is infinitely greater. And it does not define it completely because human Desire also essentially contains other modes that are opposed to those of reason. These other modes are the passionate affects, on account of which men are guided not by Reason but by their "impulses".

Let us turn to the second demonstration of IVP37 and analyse in the same way the chain of presuppositions that lies behind it. (These are essentially IIIP29–35 and IVP32–34.) The first thing we notice is that this second line of argument is concerned precisely with the "other" of human reason, that is, with the mechanism of the passions (Joy and Sadness, Hope and Fear, Love and Hatred). The passions do not express the individual's power to preserve himself by achieving a relative supremacy over external causes; on the contrary, they express his relative submission to those same causes. They are a sign not of the adequate knowledge that man may acquire of what is useful to him, but of the image he forms of what might be useful to him through his ignorance of his own nature. The life of the passions, like that of reason, is similarly conditioned by the struggle to persevere in being; like reason, the passions express a natural (though inadequate) mode of human Desire. Does this mean that the passions, which are a constant cause of conflict between men, *represent the antithesis of sociability*? *Not at all.* What Spinoza demonstrates is that *there is another form of the genesis* (or "production") *of society*, which springs from the passions themselves and which is worked out *in them and through them*, even if, in this case, the result is not necessarily a harmonious society. Let us look more closely at this chain of thought.

What is the burden of IVP32–34? Essentially this: insofar as men are subject to their passions (which express contradictory "affects"), men have nothing in common but a powerlessness, a "negation". They cannot be said to agree with one another naturally, for there is no object which has the same utility for all of them. Moreover, this situation corresponds for each man to the case of greatest possible uncertainty and instability. Not only do men in this situation not agree with one another, but they are not in agreement with themselves. Here, the reader may think that Spinoza is treating us to the sort of generalities that can be found in the work of any moralist. But in the *Ethics*, considerations such as these are rooted in an analysis of the psychic economy of Sadness (IVP34 and schol.). Sadness is the individual's consciousness of his own impotence, which leads to hatred both of the self and of others. Men would not be sad, they would not hate themselves and each other, if they were totally isolated from one another. Indeed, they would not hate one another at all if they did not feel fear on account of the love they have for a certain object and did not hope to be rid of those external causes that make them fear for their love, foremost amongst which are other men. Men hate each other insofar as they love the same object in different ways, or love incompatible objects, or (more fundamentally) imagine in different ways those objects which they all love. (It is this final difference which constitutes the singularity of their "natures".)

At this point, a surprising idea begins to emerge: that hatred is not only a social (or relational) passion but a form (however contradictory) of the "social bond", of sociability. In order to understand how this thesis might be justified, we must go back to IIIP31, the crucial proposition on which the second demonstration of the "foundations of the City" rests:

> If we imagine that someone loves, desires, or hates something we ourselves love, desire, or hate, we shall thereby love, desire, or hate it with greater constancy. But if we imagine that he is averse to what we love, or the opposite [that he loves what we hate],[2] then we shall undergo vacillation of mind.
>
> Dem.: Simply because we imagine that someone loves something, we thereby love the same thing (by P27). But we suppose that we already love it without this [cause of love]; so there is added to the love a new cause, by which it is further encouraged. As a result, we shall love what we love with greater constancy.
>
> Next, from the fact that we imagine someone to be averse to something, we shall be averse to it (by P27). But if we suppose that at the same time we love it, then at the same time we shall both love and be averse to the same thing, or (see P17S) we shall undergo vacillation of mind, QED.
>
> Cor.: From this and from P28 it follows that each of us strives, so far as he can, that everyone should love what he loves, and hate what he hates. . . .
>
> Schol.: This striving [conatus] to bring it about that everyone should approve his love and hate is really ambition (see P29S). And so we see that each of us, by his nature, wants the others to live according to his temperament [ingenium]; when all alike want this, they are alike an obstacle to one another, and when all wish to be praised, or loved, by all, they hate one another.

Three ideas are closely interrelated in this passage, and it is their interrelationship that is original and powerful. The first is the idea of identification, the fundamental psychic mechanism that communicates affects from one individual to another via the images of those individuals. The second is the idea of ambivalence, which threatens from the outset to undermine the affects of Joy and Sadness, and love and hatred along with them, and which makes the soul (or the heart: animus) of each man fluctuate. The third idea is that of the fear of difference, through which each man tries to overcome this fluctuation, and which in return only serves to maintain him indefinitely in that state.

---

[2] This is a variant from the Dutch translation of Spinoza's works published at the same time as the Latin. – TRANS.

This analysis is extremely important, for it displaces the whole problem of sociability onto a new ground. Our "fellow man" – that other individual with whom we can identify, towards whom we have "altruistic" feelings, whom religion refers to as our "neighbour" and politics as our "fellow citizen" – does not exist as such naturally, in the sense of a being who is simply there, who is given. Rather, he is constituted by a process of imaginary identification, which Spinoza calls the "imitation of the affects" (*affectuum imitatio*) (IIIP27). This process is at work both in mutual recognition between individuals and in the formation of the "multitude" as an unstable aggregate of individual passions. It follows then that men, insofar as they have "the same nature", are not alike! But they can become so. What provokes this process of identification is an "external cause", which is the *image of the other* as object of the affects. But this image is also profoundly ambivalent: it is both attractive and repulsive, reassuring and threatening.

A *single cause* is thus the origin of the antithetical patterns of behaviour through which Love and Hatred respectively are "social- ised" (IIIP32S). The first of these patterns of behaviour is Human Kindness ("a desire to do what pleases men and not do what displeases them", IIIDXLIII), which is close to Compassion ("love, insofar as it so affects a man that he is glad at another's good fortune, and saddened by his ill fortune", IIIDXXIV). The oppos- ing pattern is determined by Ambition ("excessive desire for esteem ... by which all the affects are encouraged and strengthened", IIIDXLIV; "striving to do something (and also to omit doing something) solely to please men ..., especially when we strive so eagerly to please the people [*vulgus*] that we do or omit certain things to our own injury, or another's", IIIP29S). It is Ambition which is able to bring it about that, for a time at least, men have the same tastes, the same morals, judgements or opinions (IIIP29S). It is in this way that a common good, that is, a common object of love, can be imagined. But such a common good will by definition, be inseparable from fear and hatred, that is, from the imagining of a common evil (or misfortune) to be avoided, or of the harm that would result if others were to pursue their own good in their own way. (This argument should be compared with the idea of "theological hatred" in the *TTP*.)

Thanks to these two parallel demonstrations, we are now able to grasp the remarkable complexity of the "foundations of the City". By definition, rational knowledge of the Good as common utility is not ambivalent and is not at risk of collapsing into its opposite (nor of becoming a cause of Sorrow, having been a cause for Joy). However, each man's striving to see others "live according to his temperament", or to live himself "according to the temperament of others", necessarily fluctuates between love and hatred. *Sociability is therefore the unity of a real agreement and an imaginary ambivalence, both of which have real effects.* Or, to put it another way, the unity of contraries – of rational identity *and* affective variability, but also of the irreducible singularity of individuals *and* the "similarity" of human behaviour – is nothing other than what we refer to as society. The classical concept of the "social bond" and the alternative between nature and human institutions are thus rendered wholly inadequate. This is what is demonstrated in IVP37S. For such a unity effectively to exist, there must be an authority (*potestas*) which can polarise the affects of individuals and direct their movements of love and hatred by defining once and for all the common meaning of good and evil, right and wrong, and by fixing the form through which men can ensure their own preservation by combining their individual strengths. In a word, *a Society must also be a State* (here, *civitas*). These two concepts must correspond to a single reality. We cannot claim that men are sociable "in their origins", but they *are* always already socialised. We cannot say that the State is "against nature", nor can we represent it either as a pure construction of reason or as the projection of a general order of nature onto human affairs. Society and State constitute a single relationship, at once imaginary and rational, through which the natural singularity of human individuals is expressed.

What Is Obedience?

Throughout Spinoza's oeuvre, whether in the *TTP*, the *TP* or the *Ethics*, the fundamental social relationship is always the production of obedience, and the history of States is the history of the fate of this relationship. Are we now in a position to offer a complete definition of this concept? How are we ultimately to situate the meaning of a philosophy that declares both that society is the State, therefore that society is obedience, and that freedom can only be achieved within the limits of society? Might we not be dealing with an indirect apology for some form of "voluntary slavery"?

Before we try to answer these questions, we should look again at certain propositions in the *Ethics* which have, quite rightly, always been at the heart of the debate over the meaning of Spinoza's work. We have seen how Spinoza displaced the classical argument of institutions versus nature. In the same way, and for closely related reasons, he also shifted the discussion of slavery versus freedom onto new ground. There was a tradition that extended from Aristotle to Descartes, and that was far from being exhausted, according to which the relationship of obedience that renders certain men subject to others (the slave to his master, the wife to her husband, children to their father, subjects to their prince) had to be understood in the light of the body's obedience to the soul, that is, in the light of the "voluntary" power of the soul (or mind) over the body.[3] To command is first of all to *will* and to "subjugate" bodies to one's will. Obedience is to move one's body according to an idea that the soul has formed in recognition of the will of another, and which it has made its own, whether voluntarily or under constraint. Yet this matter remains an enigma, for how does the soul act upon the body? How does it "command" its movements?

To this apparently insoluble question, Spinoza provides a radical answer: the soul does not act upon the body, any more than the body acts upon the soul. "The body cannot determine the soul to thinking, and the soul cannot determine the body to motion, to rest, or to anything else (if there is anything else)" (*Ethics*, IIIP2; translation modified). It is true that it is most unlikely

> that men can be induced to consider [these things] fairly ... They are so firmly persuaded that the body now moves, now is at rest, solely from the soul's command, and that it does a great many things which depend only on the soul's will and its art of thinking. For indeed, no

---

[3] In the first version of the *Social Contract*, Rousseau restated this point of view: "Just as in the constitution of man, the action of the soul on the body is the stumbling block of philosophy, so the action of the general will on the power of the State is the stumbling block of politics in the constitution of the State. It is here that all legislators have come to grief". See *The Social Contract*, trans. Maurice Cranston (London: Penguin, 1968), Book III, Chapter I.

one has yet determined what the body can do . . . from the laws of Nature alone. . . . So it follows that when men say that this or that action of the body arises from the soul, which has power [*imperium*] over the body, they do not know what they are saying, and they do nothing but confess, in fine-sounding words, that they are ignorant of the true causes of that action. . . . (IIIP25)

However, it must be admitted that, given the way in which Spinoza has analysed natural causality (IIP7–9, 21 and schol.), the sequence (the "order and connexion") of ideas in the soul is *the same* as the sequence of the movements of the body, and that every increase in the power of the soul over its own passions corresponds to an increase in the power of the body (IIP13S, P39C; IIIP11ff.; VP39). Let us admit this proposition as an axiom. Its demonstration depends upon Spinoza's conception of nature, in which "soul" and "body" are not two distinct "substances" but "one and the same thing" (in this case, one and the same individual). This individual is sometimes conceived of as a complex of ideas (in Spinoza's terms, "under the attribute of thought", see IIP7), sometimes as a material complex ("under the attribute of extension"). Thus, the soul is defined as the *idea of the body* (IIP11–13, 15–21; IIIP3). The major critical consequence of this argument is that instead of imagining a soul that is active insofar as the body is passive, and vice versa, we must now imagine an activity, or a passivity, that belongs simultaneously to both body and soul. How does this unifying anthropological thesis, which eliminates all notion of hierarchy, sit with Spinoza's analysis of sociability and the State?

In the *TTP*, constancy of obedience was associated with an "internal act of the soul" (*TTP*, 251; translation modified). Besides this general observation, the early text also offered a long description of obedience as a behaviour, a way of life or, better, a praxis (*TTP*, 112ff., 266ff.). What goes to make up this praxis? First, bodily movements are ordered according to fixed rituals, a collective discipline which periodically brings the body back to the same basic postures, reinforcing its habits through present sensation. In parallel, within the soul, sequences of ideas are ordered according to models of action and thought that are provided by historical and moral stories, which are considered as revealed truths. Discipline and memory, or repetition and temporal imagination, thus constitute the two opposing aspects of a single scenario. They are consequences of the same affective complex, formed from a combination of fear and hope, threats and promises, punishment and reward. To obey (but also its contrary, to disobey, to transgress the law) is to be ruled at all times by this affective complex.

In the propositions of the *Ethics*, this analysis is taken up and considerably extended. To say that obedience implies fear and hope is to say that the subject who obeys – his body and soul unified in a single "desire" – imagines a power that is superior to himself. If he is to obey *constantly*, the power of the subject who commands his obedience must appear to him to be *as great as possible*. In which case, it is not enough that he should feel fear, or even that he should conceive of a will that is the author of this law. He must imagine the subject who commands as omnipotent, and above all as omnipotent with respect to himself. Then the orders he receives from this subject will not allow for any indecision on his part, and even though they may vary, they will remain beyond question. In other words, this subject must be imagined to be "free", that is, free from any external determination. But when men thus imagine a free power, they are thinking first of themselves, then of other men (still according to their idea of themselves), and finally of God, conceived as a sovereign power on the model of man. No imaginary object could be more ambivalent.

> Given an equal cause of love, love toward a thing will be greater if we imagine the thing to be free than if we imagine it to be necessary. And similarly for hate.
> Dem.: A thing we imagine to be free must be perceived through itself, without others (by ID7). So if we imagine it to be the cause of joy or sadness, we shall thereby love or hate it (by P13S), and shall do so with the greatest love or hate that can arise from the given affect (by P48). But if we should imagine as necessary the thing which is the cause of this affect, then (by the same ID7) we shall imagine it to be the cause of the affect, not alone, but with others. And so (by P48) our love or hate toward it will be less. (IIIP49)

If we imagine the subject who commands us to be free in this sense, then we will hold him solely responsible for the good and evil that befall us through our obedience. Thus, *imagining the freedom of the other* multiplies the ambivalent consequences of our obedience *to men*. This explains why the attitude of the masses towards those who govern alternates between adulation and contempt. It also explains, *a contrario*, why the most stable State is that in which the citizens have every reason to believe (because of the very form of the institutions and the way in which they function) that those who govern them are not "all-powerful" but are in fact *determined* in their decisions by a general necessity.

What is more, this also explains the ambivalence that character-ises the effects of religion. When we imagine God as a Lawgiver or a Master whom we cannot possibly hate (save at the price of an unbearable anxiety), the uncertainty that is produced by the contrary movements of this affect (IIIP18 and schol.) is displaced, as is the hatred that exists alongside love (IIIP17 and schol.). Thus, instead of God, ourselves and our fellow men become the objects of a hatred that has no limits. This is the origin of the sadness that characterises religion, of humility and "theological hatred". On the other hand, the definition of reason itself is to conceive of *God as necessary*, that is, as Nature itself in its impersonal totality. If we do so, all fear and all "anger" disappear. The love we then feel for God is what the fifth part of the *Ethics* calls an "intellectual love of God", that is, both knowledge and the desire for knowledge (VP20 and P32–33). We no longer see God as the subject who commands us, and in return we are able to love our fellow men, not as subjects whom we endow with a fictive freedom, nor as creatures who obey or disobey their creator, but as those natural beings who are most useful to us and therefore most necessary. Paradoxically, to see them in this way frees both ourselves and our fellow men as far as is possible from dependence on the passions. Spinoza calls this state of mutual freedom *friendship* (IVP70–73).

These two ideas – thinking of God as necessary, on the one hand, and loving men and seeking out their friendship because of the reciprocal relation of utility that exists between them and ourselves, on the other – have immediate ethical implications. Moreover, they are inseparable, because on the practical level they both determine one and the same relationship between the bodies concerned. This relationship is one in which obedience tends to cancel itself out through its own effects, as love and reason gradually gain the upper hand over fear and superstition. These two ideas already underlay the arguments of the *TTP* and the *TP*, albeit in different ways. In describing the organisation of a democratic society, in which the sovereign (acting out of his own self-interest) guaranteed freedom of expression and religion took the form of a universal faith that has been interiorised by every individual, Spinoza was describing what we recognise now as a limiting case of this relationship. All discipline, and with it all fear of punishment, was on the side of the State, but at the same time this discipline *tended* to coincide with the collective construction of the common interest (which is why it took a contractual form). All hope, on the other hand, and with it all belief in narratives of salvation, lay on the side of (true) religion, but at the same time this hope *tended* to coincide with the immediate certainty that accompanies virtuous acts and love for one's neighbour. These two "rules of conduct" (*ratio vitae*) (*TTP*, 101, 208–9, 217–18, etc.) did not, however, simply meld into one. Rather, we might say that they exchanged their forms of action: on the one side, the form of law and commandment; on the other, the affective power of love between men. Because Christians are also citizens living in a State, they come to see their inner faith (*fides*) as a law; because the citizens are also believers who see each other as "neighbours", their obedience to the law also takes the form of a constant loyalty (*fides*).

However, this subtle arrangement may still strike us as deeply equivocal. The collective norm of obedience has not been abolished; on the contrary, since it turns out in the final analysis to consist in the conformity of actions to a rule, whatever may be the motives and the means by which this conformity is achieved (*TTP*, 251–2). But, in practice, it is necessary to ensure that the conflicts and the violence that would be produced by our imagining the freedom of others are neutralised, so that each individual may accede to the greatest possible effective freedom. For this to be the case, we have to assume that the mass of men have already collectively mastered their own passions, that they have already achieved their own "internal" liberation. Is this not simply a utopian delusion, a way of supposing that the problem we are confronted with has in fact been solved in advance?

It is significant that from the outset the *TP* refuses this appeal to utopia, by emphasising the irreducible antithesis between the notions of obedience and freedom (*TP*, IV, 5). To pass off obedience as such as freedom would be an exercise in mystification. True freedom is synonymous with power and independence, while obedience always implies a form of dependency. But here again a remarkable dialectic is set in motion. Reason, in itself, does not "command" anything, but it does show that an ordered State, which is capable of ensuring its own preservation, is the condition of any effective progress towards utility. Individuals who are guided by reason must therefore will the existence of such a State, which they would obey in the same way as every other citizen. Reciprocally, the "absolute" State, in the sense we have already defined, will tend above all to its own preservation. From this point of view, it is of course a matter of indifference whether the obedience of individuals is motivated by fear or by love. But in order to ensure that their obedience is constant, the State must guarantee their security and its own domestic peace, and must on no account threaten to strip them of the irreducible minimum of their individuality. As we have seen, the whole organisation of the "absolute" State is intended to induce those men who are guided by their passions to act *as if* they were guided by reason (*TP*, X, 4–6). In this sense, collective rationality can be said to include as the condition of its possibility both the obedience of the least reasonable individuals and that of the most reasonable, whether those individuals govern or are governed. It is this common rule which gives knowledge (or reason) some purchase on the passions of the multitude. If every individual remained by himself, reason would have no power over them.

Thus we can see that the propositions which deal with obedience and the transcendence of obedience make no sense at the level of the isolated individual, save perhaps as a provisional abstraction. "Sequences" of ideas, like sequences of bodily movements, bind together all the individuals in nature, each with his neighbour, even if the way in which they are thus determined can never be grasped in its entirety. When an individual is passive, it is because his soul has been subjugated by the circulation of the affects and by the "general ideas" that inhabit the collective imagination (according to the process of affective "imitation" described above). His body too will have been simultaneously subjugated by the unrestrained influence of all the surrounding bodies. When an individual is active, there is on the contrary a coherent order structuring the encounters between his body and other bodies, and the ideas that are in his soul follow on from one another according to "common notions" – in the double sense of common to all men and common to both men and nature as a whole, that is to say, objective. *In both cases, we are dealing with modes of communication: the very form which individuality takes is thus the result of a given mode of communication.* With this notion, we come to what is perhaps the most profound of all Spinoza's ideas.

"Ethics" and Communication

To recapitulate: in classical terms, there are three problems connected with obedience to the law. What is its psychic (or psychosomatic) mechanism? What is the relationship between obedience, fear (or constraint) and love? And how does obedience relate to knowledge? (What relationships does it create between the "wise" and the "ignorant", between knowledge and power?) For Spinoza, these three questions are in reality a single problem to which there is a single answer. Passion and reason are both, in the final analysis, modes of communication between bodies and between ideas of bodies. In the same way, political regimes should be thought of as orders of communication: some of them are conflictual and unstable, others are coherent and stable. Or rather, in some of them the conflictual aspect tends to overwhelm their coherence, while in others coherence tends to prove stronger than the pull of conflict.

In fact, any real State contains within itself both of these tendencies. It therefore also contains the two limiting states that Spinoza defines through the hypotheses of "barbarity", on the one hand, and a community of men "guided by Reason", on the other. Gathered together in fear of a common master, whose power is at once real and imaginary (and more imaginary than real), and who himself lives in fear of those who fear him, individuals commune in the same affects. They are both fascinated and repelled by their fellow men, but they have no true common object. Their communication, therefore, is minimal, however much noise it generates, and this state of society differs only in name from a "state of nature". In these conditions, multitude is a synonym for solitude (*TP*, V, 4; VI, 4), and any apparent unanimity cannot long survive so much latent antagonism. The City, on the other hand, however repressive it may be, always already includes "something [held] in common" (*Ethics*, IVP29). Where there is as yet no common good (that good which the young Spinoza, as early as the *Treatise on the Emendation of the Intellect*, had referred to as a "communicable good", without being able to spell out all the implications of this phrase), each man nevertheless begins to increase his strength as far as possible by building on the strength of others. In this way, an objective solidarity begins to take shape. Since no individual is rigorously "like" any other, each having his own "temperament", multitude is then synonymous with exchange (in the broadest possible sense – exchange of properties is only one aspect of this idea) and with free communication between irreducibly singular beings.

The result is a permanent tension between two sequences of ideas and of movements. *But this tension has no meaning as long as we imagine it as a static confrontation.* In fact, it is nothing other than the struggle of individuals who have no pre-established goal to transform their own collective "temperament". At this point, it becomes clear that it would be a mistake to interpret Spinoza's notion of the "preservation" of the body politic as ideologically conservative. On the contrary, the more the body politic, that individual of individuals, develops its own powers, the more the real-imaginary complexity of social relationships as Spinoza conceives it is revealed as a principle of mobility. Obedience itself (and its correlative representation, the "law"), as it is institutionalised by the State, religion and morality, is not an immutable given but the fulcrum of a continual transition. Or, more precisely, since progress is never guaranteed, it is what is at stake in a praxis (a struggle?) whose decisive moment is the transformation of the mode of communication itself.

Spinoza defines this praxis as a striving on the part of individuals to bring about *rationally* those actions to which they are usually determined by their passions. This they can do by representing to themselves the necessity of those actions (*Ethics*, IVP59). The most effective form of communication is that which is achieved by means of rational knowledge. Individual reason by itself is too weak and must therefore always have recourse to passions that are bad in themselves (that is, are causes of sadness, such as glory, ambition, humility, and so on). In this way, one affect can be used to overcome another, and discipline can be imposed upon the multitude (*Ethics*, IVP55 and P58). But knowledge is a process by which communication is continuously being improved. It can multiply the power of every individual, even if some individuals inevitably know more than others. We are as far here from the idea of the "philosopher king" (or from any attribution of power to the guardians of knowledge) as we are from the idea of "salvation through knowledge", that is, knowledge as a speculative fortress against the evils of the world. Both these ideas share the assumption that, to paraphrase Spinoza, knowledge and praxis relate to one another as numerically distinct powers, as if knowledge were a "State within the State". Spinoza was all too familiar with the use (and perversion) of knowledge in regimes organised around "theocratic" superstition, and he *never* claimed that rational knowledge could, as such, establish and justify the obedience of those who are ignorant to those who are wise. If knowledge did come to perform this function, it would be reduced to a new form of superstition, with philosophers and scientists as its theologians and high priests.

But the *TTP* had already pointed out in passing that language contains at least one element whose integrity cannot be destroyed by the manipulations of the theologians. The meaning of words is immune to such corruption. Because "a language is preserved by the learned and unlearned alike" (*TTP*, 148), the meaning of its words is therefore determined by the common usage of those words by both the "learned" and the "unlearned", insofar as there is communication between them.

The *Ethics* helps us to build on this notation through its analysis of the form of the successive "types of knowledge" (imagination, scientific reason and "intellectual love of God"). Knowledge begins with our use of the words of the language, in descriptions and stories. This first genre is inadequate by its very nature, for its operative principle is to summarise the irreducible experience of each individual (sensations, memories, affects) under a series of *common nouns* which stand for abstract and general notions (*Ethics*, IIP40 and schol.). The rational knowledge provided by the last two genres does not, however, lead us away from this common element of language and into an incommunicable "vision", though Spinoza still uses the old term *intuitive knowledge* to refer to the explanation of singular objects by their immanent causes. Rather, a form of intellectual work enables primary usage to be corrected, so that the sequence of words accurately reflects relationships of natural necessity (IIP18S; VP1). By this process, words come to refer to *common notions*. This allows us to define more precisely the place of knowledge in the life of the multitude. If no man ever thinks alone, then we might say that to know really is to think ever less by oneself. The truth of this does not depend on which individuals have access to true ideas. Moreover, every individual has at least "one true idea", even if it is only the idea of what is useful to him, which contains the seed of the equation between freedom and the power to act. This idea can be logically connected to the ideas of others (IIP43 and 47). Thus political society contains an immanent power through which it can be transformed so as to become the context of a life that is properly "human", a life that is lived with joy.

Because life in society is a communicative activity, knowledge has *two* practical dimensions: one of which relates to conditions, and the other to effects. If we agree with Spinoza – and to the extent that we do agree – that communication is structured by relationships of ignorance and knowledge, superstition, and ideological antagonism, which are invested with human desire and which express an activity of our bodies themselves, then we must also agree that knowledge is a praxis, and that the struggle for knowledge (that is, philosophy) is a political praxis. Without this praxis, the decision-making processes that converge upon democracy, as described in the *TP*, would be simply unintelligible. In this way, we can see why the essential element in Spinoza's conception of democracy is freedom of communication. We can also see why the theory of the "body politic" is neither a straightforward "physics" of power, nor a psychological analysis of the submission of the masses, nor a method for formalising a juridical order, but the search for a strategy of collective liberation, whose guiding motto would be *as many as possible, thinking as much as possible* (*Ethics*, VP5–10). Thus, finally, we see why the set purpose of the philosopher – his "ethic" – is not to prepare or announce the revolution but to take the risk of thinking in full view of his public. That is not a risk that many revolutions have been prepared to take.

5

POLITICS AND COMMUNICATION

As we have seen, the different modalities of communication occupy a central place in Spinoza's argument in the *Ethics*. In this final chapter,[1] I want both to explore this theme further and to go back over certain of the main conclusions I have reached so far. My purpose in doing so is to show how the whole of Spinoza's philosophy, insofar as it makes metaphysics inseparable from politics (this unity or reciprocal presupposition being precisely what is meant here by an "ethic"), can be understood as a highly original philosophy of communication.

Disagreement over the interpretation of Spinoza's philosophy has always centred on three main questions:

1. *The question of nature*: Spinoza is now famous, and was once notorious, for having identified "God" and "nature" (*Deus sive natura*), and for having described all reality as a "mode" of this unique substance.[2] Was his philosophy therefore a form of

---

[1] This fifth chapter, which did not figure in the original French edition of *Spinoza and Politics*, is based on a lecture given to an audience of philosophy teachers at the University of Créteil and originally published in the journal *Questions de philosophie*, no. 39, June 1989.

[2] The expression *Deus sive natura* rapidly became, and to some extent still is, a motto which was held to summarise the essence of Spinoza's thinking. Three qualifications are necessary, however. First, although this phrase perfectly sums up the doctrines set out in the first part of the *Ethics* (if we understand *Deus* and *Natura* as two equivalent "names" for the infinite substance), it does not actually appear in the text of the *Ethics* until the preface to part IV. This does not reduce its importance, but it does show that Spinoza's use of it is contextual, as the perfect antidote to the system of "human bondage" which is the subject of this section. Second, it can be seen as a displacement or reversal of those "tautological" formulae which are the paramount (and totalitarian) expression of the theological and theological-political ideologies: "God is God", "The law is the law". This is the origin of its subversive power. Third, the appearance of this phrase is not unprecedented but in fact constitutes the final stage of a lengthy history. The two most important preceding stages were, on the one hand, the Stoics' and Neo-Stoics' use of the symmetrical and properly

pantheism? Was it a radically mechanistic vision? And doesn't such a thesis lead inevitably to an absurdity, that is, to the liquidation of all moral values? Bayle was among the first to ironise on this theme: "in Spinoza's system all those who say *the Germans killed ten thousand Turks* speak badly and falsely, unless they mean by that, *God modified into Germans killed God modified into ten thousand Turks*."[3]

2. *The question of man*: what is Spinoza's anthropology? What we have just said points towards a first aporia, for in such a naturalistic perspective human reality would seem to be necessarily deprived of all autonomy. Spinoza goes on to assert a strict correlation between the soul and the body, since the former is merely "the idea" of the latter. (This position is generally referred to as "parallelism", even though this term does not appear in Spinoza's writings and is in any case equivocal in its meaning.)[4] Yet none of this prevents Spinoza from describing human perfection as intellectual knowledge and the achievement of freedom.

3. *The question of right*: in his explicitly political works, Spinoza proposes that right is nothing other than power (that of the individual or that of the collectivity): "For example, fish are determined by nature to swim, and the big ones to eat the smaller ones. Thus it is by sovereign natural right that fish inhabit water, and the big ones eat the smaller ones" (*TTP*, 237). He then immediately claims that this definition contains within itself a

---

pantheistic formula *Natura sive Deus* (see Jacqueline Lagrée, *Juste Lipse et la restauration du stoicisme* [Paris: Librairie Vrin, 1994], pp. 52ff.) and, on the other, the sixth of Descartes' *Meditations*, "For by nature considered in general, I understand here nothing else but God himself [*per naturam . . . nihil nunc aliud quam vel Deum ipsum*], or the order and arrangement [*coordinationem*] that God has established among created things" (Descartes, *Meditations, Synopsis*, in *The Philosophical Writings of Descartes*, trans. John Cottingham, Robert Stoothoft and Dugald Murdoch [Cambridge: Cambridge University Press, 1984], vol. VII, p. 64).

[3] Pierre Bayle, "Spinoza", remark N.IV in the *Dictionnaire historique et critique* (1696), cited in Bayle, *Écrits sur Spinoza*, texts chosen and presented by Françoise Charles-Daubert and Pierre-François Moreau (Paris: L'autre Rive – Berg International Editeur, 1983), p. 69.

[4] The term "parallelism" seems to have been invented by Leibniz, who applied it to his own theory of the correspondence between the soul and the body, which was based on the doctrine of "pre-established harmony". By a strange misunderstanding, which would merit detailed analysis, it later came to be used by historians of philosophy to refer principally to Spinoza's conception of the *identity* between the "order and connection" of thought and that of extension: *Ethics*, IIP7 and schol. Cf. G. Deleuze, *Spinoza et le problème de l'expression* (Paris: Editions de Minuit, 1968), p. 95.

foundation for freedom, in this case civil freedom, as it exists in and through the State. Yet this claim is far from straightforward, as his two main political works (the *TTP* and the *TP*) show when they draw substantially different conclusions from this single principle. Where the one argues for the limitation of the State, the other defends its absolute character. In these conditions it is hardly surprising that their theoretical heritage has been so various, the *TTP* being to theoreticians of the *Rechtsstaat* ("State of right") what the *TP* is to proponents of the *Machtsstaat* ("State of force"). In this way, the two terms that were paradoxically unified by Spinoza's definition are separated once again, or if not separated, then interpreted as privileging one over the other.

In this concluding chapter, I shall not try to solve all these problems. But I do want to show how light can be shed on them by interrogating the consequences of the idea that Spinoza's philosophy is, in a strong sense of the term, a philosophy of *communication* – or, even better, of *modes of communication* – in which the theory of knowledge and the theory of sociability are closely intertwined. Spinoza himself addressed this idea in his theory of "common notions". By this concept, he was referring simultaneously to the universality of reason and to the institution of a collectivity. Common notions are the true ideas that underlie any demonstrative science and that are "equally in the part and in the whole" (*Ethics*, IIP37), that is to say, are inherent to human nature in particular as they are to natural causality in general. They are also common to all men insofar as they come together to live and to think, whatever their degree of wisdom or their social condition. It is this fundamental notion which we must now analyse if we want to grasp more fully the relationship between the function and forms of the State, the definition of individuality and the true nature of freedom. In this way, we will see how the problem that provided Spinoza with his theoretical premise turns out to be also the practical objective of his philosophy.

Power and Freedom

The theme of communication is already present in the first text that can with any certainty be attributed to Spinoza, the *Treatise on the Emendation of the Intellect* (*TRE*), which was written circa 1660. It begins thus:

> After experience had taught me that all things which regularly occur in ordinary life are empty and futile ... I resolved at last to try and find out whether there was anything which would be the true good, capable of communicating itself [*verum bonum, et sui communicabile*], and which alone would affect the mind, all others being rejected – whether there was something which, once found and acquired, would continously give me the greatest joy, to eternity. (*TRE*, 1)

This good turns out to be nothing other than knowledge or, to put it in Spinoza's own terms, the true idea of singular things. Its acquisition seems to depend above all on a moral and intellectual ascesis, which Spinoza calls the "true life". We are certainly meant to understand that those men who aspire to such knowledge will find themselves drawn into a free and equal community with one another (that is, friendship). But it is difficult to think of such a community as anything other than a retreat from political realities. Yet there is no sign of any such retreat in the three great works of Spinoza's maturity, the *TTP*, the *Ethics* and the *TP*. They may differ greatly in content and in style, but they are all three simultaneously works of philosophy *and* political inquiries. One of the most original aspects of Spinoza's thought, as we have already shown, is to have abolished the separations and hierarchical order that used to exist between the different domains of knowledge. In this, his approach to philosophy was completely new, and to this day has found few disciples. His work is not divided into a metaphysics (or an ontology) on the one hand and a politics or an ethics, which are seen as "secondary" applications of "first" philosophy, on the other. From the very beginning, his metaphysics is a philosophy of praxis, of activity; and his politics is a philosophy, for it constitutes the field of experience in which human nature acts and strives to achieve liberation. It is necessary to insist on this point, which has often been misunderstood. Spinoza's works have too often been cut in two: "metaphysicians" busied themselves with the *Ethics*, which they placed in the great sequence of ontologies and theories of knowledge that stretches from Plato to Descartes, Kant and Hegel, while "political scientists" concentrated on the two treatises, which they classed with the works of Locke,

Hobbes, Grotius and Rousseau as the classical theories of natural right and the State. As a result, the fact that the very core of the *Ethics* is an analysis of sociability has remained largely unexplored. Yet without this analysis, Spinoza's definitions of right and the State would be unintelligible.

Both the *TTP* and the *TP* begin with identical definitions of right as power. This definition is universal: it applies to the individual's right, the right of the State, the right of Nature as a whole and of all its parts. It is not simply a definition, it is a thesis: *every right is limited* (except for the right of God), but its limits have nothing to do with either a prohibition or an obligation. They are simply the limits *of a real power*. Taken to its logical consequences, this principle is extraordinarily subversive. Its total realism undermines absolutely any pretensions to an authority that would be superior to the interests of individuals. A State which cannot impose its authority on its subjects, either by constraint or by consensus, has no right over them, and thus no right to exist. Contracts of every sort have no validity beyond the benefits that the different parties may derive from them. But, at the same time, an individual can claim no right over and against the State, except for that which he is able, alone or with others, to enforce. The most powerful State is also that which has the most extensive right. But experience shows that this State is not the authoritarian State, much less a State that rules by violence, and which will, sooner or later, be overthrown by violence. It is the reasonable State which commands the greatest obedience, because it "reigns over the souls of its subjects" (*TTP*, 251; translation modified), that is, because it obtains each man's inner loyalty to the public order. Likewise, the most powerful individual is also the individual who has the most extensive right. But he is not the individual who, by some unsustainable fiction, contrives to live in total isolation from (or opposition to) all other men. Isolation is synonymous with poverty, and antagonism implies a system of reciprocal threat and constraint. The right of the individual, like that of the State, consists rather of all that he is effectively able to do (and think) in a given situation.

All of which amounts to saying that the idea of a "theoretical right", conceived along the lines of a capacity or an authority that might exist independently of its being exercised, is absurd. Every right is defined in relation to a concrete reality, because it corresponds to the activity of one or more individuals. This explains why Spinoza was keen to distance himself from Hobbes on this fundamental point, for in Hobbes's thought "Law, and Right, differ as much, as Obligation and Liberty",[5] and natural rights must give way to civil rights. Nature must be replaced by an artificial juridical order if there is to be security and safety between men of opposing interests. "With regard to political theory, the difference between Hobbes and myself, which is the subject of your inquiry, consists in this, that I always preserve the natural right in its entirety, and I hold that the sovereign power in a State has right over a subject only in proportion to the excess of its power over that of a subject. That is always the case in a state of nature" (*The Letters*, L, p. 258). We should remember that the sovereign, for Spinoza, may take any form, may be a monarch or the citizen body (who are thus their own "subjects"). Whether there is conflict or collaboration between powers, inequality of birth or civic equality, civil war or domination by foreign powers, every concrete situation is determined, to different degrees, by natural right. Thus there is no contradiction between positive rights and natural rights. Indeed, not only do the former *not* replace the latter, but insofar as they are effective they are identical with them.[6]

This conception of right will have three particularly important consequences:

1. The freedom of the individual, whoever he may be, and inasmuch as it has not been reduced to a purely formal pretension, may be endangered both by his internal weaknesses and by external enemies. The individual who is *sui juris* (independent) is not exempted from observing the law, but he is not *constrained* (or only as little as possible) by others and by the general law.

2. The notion of a state of nature as it was conceived by the classical theoreticians, that is, as an origin, whether historic or

---

[5] Thomas Hobbes, *Leviathan*, ed. Richard Tuck (Cambridge: Cambridge University Press, 1991), part I, chapter 14, p. 91.

[6] The effective power of positive rights is what Kelsen would later call their *Wirksamkeit*, inasmuch as they are additional to the order of legitimacy or *Rechtfertigung*. For this comparison, see Manfred Walther, "Spinoza und der Rechtspositivismus", in *Spinoza nell' 350. Anniversario della nascita*. Proceedings of the First Italian International Congress on Spinoza, ed. Emilia Giancotti (Napoli: Bibliopolis, 1985).

ideal, and whether a state of innocence (Rousseau's "noble savage") or perversity (Hobbes's *puer robustus*), tends here to be gradually deprived of its object. In the limiting case, Spinoza's argument will lead to the paradox of a *natural right without a corresponding state of nature*.

3. The "multitude" is not (as it is for Hobbes and for many others) the antithesis of the "people", to whom it is opposed as the savage state is to an ordered society. Spinoza lived at a time of considerable unrest, and he saw clearly that the problem posed by the violence of the masses (whether overt or latent) cannot be dealt with by trying to evacuate that violence, by expelling it from the common space. Rather, to come to terms with violence is the true object of politics. Yet as we shall see Spinoza came to change his mind quite considerably on this point in later years.

"Desire Is Man's Very Essence"

The theses we have been discussing contain an implicit anthropology. That is, they suggest an original answer to the age-old question: "What is man?" The *Ethics* assembles this answer, grounding it on a fundamental proposition: "Desire is man's very essence" (IIIP95). This proposition itself derives from an ontological principle: "Each thing, as far as it can, and as far as it lies in itself, strives [*conatur*] to persevere in its being" (that is, it does so as far as it can by its own power and in accord with its essence) (IIIP6; translation modified). How are we to understand these statements?

Spinoza uses the term desire (*appetitus, cupiditas*) to refer both to the individual's effort to preserve his own being (his own form) and to the peculiarly human consciousness of this effort. But he is careful to distinguish between this desire and the will. The will is the name we give to each man's effort to preserve himself when, by a fiction, we think of the soul in isolation from the body. Desire, on the other hand, is the same effort as it relates "inseparably to the soul and the body" (translation modified). To define man by his will gives us a partial and inadequate idea of what man is. Every man is a unity of soul and body. He is neither the composite of a form and a substance (as the Aristotelian tradition has it) nor the union of two substances (according to Descartes' reinterpretation of the Christian tradition). Rather, soul and body are two expressions of a single entity, that is, of one and the same individual (IIP7S). It is perhaps better for us to reverse the habitual order of these notions and to understand Spinoza's idea thus: man's unity is that of a single desire for self-preservation, which is simultaneously expressed through the actions and the passions of the body, and through the actions and passions of the soul (that is, through sequences of movements and sequences of ideas). These sequences are substantially identical, because they express the same individual essence; but they do so differently, thus expressing the irreducible multiplicity of the orders of natural causality.

This is admittedly a difficult thesis, but its polemical significance is quite clear. Spinoza rejects all the traditional forms of hierarchy between soul and body. This refusal will in effect rehabilitate the body and overturn, both in ethics and in politics, our assumptions about mastery and obedience. This is so, whether the relationship of obedience is to oneself or to an "external" authority – an individual or an idea, such as the idea of God, which is necessarily related to certain movements of the body. According to Spinoza, we do not know just how far the power of the body extends. We have therefore no reason to impose upon it arbitrary and repressive limits, and in particular no reason to forbid it from having access to knowledge. On the contrary, we should think of the soul in general as "the idea of the body" (IIP13). This idea can never be totally adequate, but its "first and principal" aspect is always "the striving . . . to affirm the existence of the body" (IIIP10D). This rehabilitation, however, is certainly not to be achieved by reducing the soul to the body, since neither is the essence or the cause of the other. Spinoza is no "spiritualist", but neither is he a materialist, at least in the usual sense of the term. He maintains, paradoxically, that because of the identity of the sequences of which they are composed, the soul can no more act upon the body than the body can act upon the soul. The mind-body problem, that major obsession running through the history of philosophy, is eliminated at a single stroke. Instead of thinking of the soul as active to the extent that the body is passive, and vice versa, we have to imagine an activity and a passivity that concern simultaneously both the soul and the body. As a result, social relationships too must be imagined as both ideological relationships (in souls) and physical relationships (in bodies) that are exactly correlated with each other and that express the same desire for self-preservation on the part of the individual, whether that desire is compatible or not with the desires of other individuals and complexes of individuals (such as the nation or the State).

Desire, as Spinoza understands it, is not the expression of a *lack*. On the contrary, it is essentially positive (since every individual in nature will tend to preserve its being and its form – indeed, this activity is its "essence"). But it is the expression of a *finitude*, a finitude we have already encountered in connection with the notion of right. For no individual has the power to preserve himself absolutely. All he can do is obstruct, with more or less success and permanence, those internal and external causes which tend to his destruction. For that reason he must pursue or escape from certain objects, which may be human (and therefore the bearers of other desires) or not, imaginary or real, objects of faith or of knowledge. A major part of Spinoza's originality is to have proposed that the object of desire is neither predetermined nor already defined, but is changeable and can be substituted. The one exception to this rule is the desire for rational knowledge (knowledge "by causes"), whose object is *any singular thing*. That is why the essential distinction here is not that between the conscious and the unconscious, but between activity and passivity, depending on whether the individual is dominated by the object on which his desire has focused or whether he becomes himself that object's "adequate cause". All the polymorphous forms of desire are nothing other than a certain degree of activity which is sufficient to overcome passivity, a (positive) differential between life and death.

Clearly, then, the term "essence" is being used here in a rather unusual sense. The contexts of the definitions I have cited above are very clear on this point: "essence" does not refer to a *general idea* of humanity, an abstract concept under which all individuals are subsumed and their differences neutralised. On the contrary, it refers precisely to the power that *singularises* each individual, conferring upon him a unique destiny. Thus, to affirm that desire is the essence of man is to affirm that every individual is irreducible in the difference of his own desire. We might say this is a form of "nominalism", since Spinoza considers the human species to be an abstraction. Only individuals *exist*, in the strong sense of the term.

But this nominalism has nothing to do with atomistic individualism: to say that all individuals are different (or, better, that they act and suffer in different ways) is not to say that they can be isolated from one another. The idea of such an isolation is simply another mystificatory abstraction. It is the relationship of each individual to other individualities and their reciprocal actions and passions which determine the form of the individual's desire and actuate its power. Singularity is a trans-individual function. It is a function of communication.

But this definition of desire has yet another consequence, for Spinoza goes on to reject the traditional distinction between knowledge and affectivity. Again, rather than reducing one aspect to the other, he displaces the terms of the debate itself. He does so by extending his critique of the notion of the will. The notion of the will is not only an abstraction, which derives from a false idea of the soul, it rests on a complete failure to understand what an idea is. An idea, or a complex of ideas, is not a picture, an image of things deposited "in the soul"; it is an action on the part of a thinking individual, who at the same time is affected by other individuals (human or not), or on the part of several individuals thinking together, that is, forming the same idea. There is therefore no reason after the event to add a special act of will or a special effect produced by an emotion in order for this idea to pass from the sphere of thought into the sphere of praxis. Every idea is always already accompanied by an affect (joy or sadness, and − as a consequence − love or hate, hope or fear, and so on). Conversely, every affect is tied to a representation (a verbal image or a concept). The strongest ideas, and in particular "adequate" ideas, which are intrinsically true, are also the strongest affects. For Spinoza, they are joyful because they are linked to man's striving to imagine those things that increase the power of his body to act and thereby the power of his soul as well (IIIP11 and schol.). But the most violent affects are those which are inherent in the most vivid images, whether they are clear and intelligible or not. When we know things adequately ("by their causes") we are not thereby cut off from the affective register; on the contrary, we tend to turn all our affects into joyful passions. Conversely, it would be entirely false to think that the life of the passions, which is characterised by "vacillation of the soul" and by inner conflict, corresponds to the absence of all knowledge; for if we are thinking (and to suffer is to think), then we also know something, albeit in the weakest possible form – that of imagining external objects on the basis of the effects they produce in us, faced with which we feel ourselves to be relatively impotent. This is, of course, an illusion or a misappreciation. But even such an illusion is not an absence of knowledge; it too is a "form of knowledge". Spinoza says that *man is always thinking* (but he does not always think adequately). We might add that he always knows something, just as he is always affected by joy or sadness at his thoughts and for the objects of his thoughts. Here Spinoza clearly anticipates Freud, whose doctrine is characterised less by the importance it places on affectivity than by the importance it places on the role of thought in affectivity.

The artificial distinction between knowledge and affectivity, which is part of the doctrine of both the intellectualist and the irrationalist, must therefore be replaced by another distinction: that between different *types of knowledge*, which correspond to different *affective regimes*. Together, these two elements form a "way of life". There are two main types of knowledge, which Spinoza refers to as imagination and reason, and which stand in opposition to each other as passive to active. Once more, we are confronted with an anthropological distinction whose political significance is immediately evident. Some men live in the world of the imagination. Spinoza is continually hinting that this is the fate of the masses, at least in most historical situations, which would explain the disturbances to which regimes founded on superstition are prone, especially theocracies and monarchies. A minority of men have access to the world of reason, thanks to their circumstances and to their personal endeavours. It would seem that, if a truly democratic regime were to be brought about, this minority would have to become a majority. However, if we look more closely at the argument of the *Ethics* and the *TTP*, we will see that this simple presentation is too mechanical. In reality, all men live in both the world of the imagination and that of reason. In every man there is already some reason (that is, some true ideas and some joyful passions), if only because of the partial knowledge he has of his own usefulness; and in every man there is still some imagination (even when he has acquired many true ideas through science and philosophy and from his own experience), if only because of his own inability to dominate all external causes (which we may collectively refer to as "fortune"). The fundamental problem of all politics, which is already the problem of political institutions and of the preservation of the State, is to know how reason and imagination interact, how they contribute to sociability. In the previous chapter, we saw how Spinoza analyses this question through a "double demonstration" and a "double commentary" (scholium) on proposition 37 in part IV of the *Ethics*, where he sets out "the foundations of the City".

The first demonstration and the first scholium explain the *rational genesis* of the City. Men who are guided by reason (and insofar as they are so guided) seek what is useful to them. What is most useful to any man is other men, whose strength, when combined with his own, will provide him with greater security, prosperity and knowledge. The desire for self-preservation therefore rationally implies, for each man, that he should desire what is good for others and want to form a stable association with them. It must be emphasised that, in line with the anthropological theses discussed above, men are reciprocally useful to one another not to the extent that they are identical and interchangeable (that each can take the place of any other and "establish the maxim of his action as a universal law", as Kant was to say some time later), but precisely insofar as they differ from each other in their "temperament" (*ingenium*), that is, in their capacities and their characters. To desire the good of others as a function of my own good (and thus to anticipate my own good through the good of others), so as to be able to use others and to be used by them, is therefore in no way to desire that those others should be like me, should act like me and adopt my opinions. On the contrary, it is to desire that they should be different, develop their own powers and know what is of use to them more and more adequately. In other words, the City that is rationally conceived and constructed through the daily activity of its members is indeed a collective individuality, bound together by the affects of friendship, morality and religion, but it is not founded on uniformity. Thus it is itself the means by which each man can affirm and strengthen his own individuality.

As we have seen, the *affective genesis* contradicts the rational genesis on one central point: for men effectively to pursue a common good, this good must be for each man an object of love in his imagination. The love which I feel for something is increased by the fact that this object is also loved (and therefore desired) by others, and is increased the more, the more people there are who love it. The convergence of all these affects and their reciprocal reinforcement of one another can constitute a form of social bond. But this simple schema needs to be qualified on two points. First, the reinforcement that is in question here is indeed an objective benefit (as we have seen above), but it rests on a mechanics of *illusion*: I imagine that others love the same thing as I do (that our love is for the same object), and that they love it in the same way (with the same love as I have). Second, this reinforcement is *ambivalent*: for it depends upon the feeling I have that I am impotent to obtain the good that I desire, on my hope that I may be able to obtain it through others and on my fear that they may deprive me of what I desire. It is therefore able to change at any moment into its contrary; indeed, it *contains its contrary*. As a result, the City that is constituted in this way rests on a psychic economy that is at once very powerful and highly unstable: this is what Spinoza calls "the imitation of affects" (*imitatio affectuum*), which, translated into modern terms, we might refer to as identification. If men were entirely reasonable creatures, the communities they form would be cemented entirely by reciprocal utility and thus by difference in similarity. But since men are all, though to differing degrees, imaginative creatures, their communities must also rely upon mechanisms of identification, that is, on an (imaginary) *excess* of similarity.

Spinoza classifies ambition among the relationships of identification. *Ambition* is the desire of individuals to see others conform to their own opinions, and to present others with an image of themselves which will please them, with which they can identify. Spinoza attributes collective representations of *class* and *nation* to the same causes (IIIP46). These cases serve to illustrate the corollaries of affective identification, namely fear and misappreciation of the differences between individuals. The analyses of the *TTP* allow us to add the Churches as a further institution of this type, or indeed any community founded on reciprocal identification among believers in a shared religious dogma. All these examples show that there is no love (for our neighbour, our fellow citizen, our companion) without hatred (class hatred, national hatred, theological hatred), and that these two contrary passions are necessarily directed not only at objects that differ from one another, but also at the same objects, as they are perceived in the imagination as similar or different. (Thus the believer will love his neighbour in God but will also fear and hate him as a sinner and a heretic.)

Sociability rooted in the passions is therefore necessarily conflictual. But it is nevertheless a *real* sociability. One of Spinoza's greatest acts of intellectual courage was to break with the traditional alternative, according to which either individuals are opposed to one another and society dissolves (*homo homini lupus*), or society is constituted as a whole, and therefore peace and love necessarily reign between its members (*homo homini deus*). Nevertheless, social hatred, now that we have admitted its existence, and all forms of affective vacillation between excessive love and excessive hatred in general, must still be kept within certain limits. These limits are imposed by the State, that is, by a power whose constraints take the form of laws. That is why, in the second scholium of proposition 37 in part IV of the *Ethics*, Spinoza deduces from the conflict of the passions the necessity for individuals to alienate part of their power (or their right) in favour of a public institution that will define good and evil, justice and injustice, piety and impiety, in universal terms; that will codify the rules of property and justice ("render to each his own"); and that will ensure that individuals receive, according to the facts of the case, punishment for their faults and reward for their merits. Thus the centre of the argument shifts from the notion of the common good to that of civil obedience.

We must therefore understand that these two antithetical narratives of the genesis of the City do not correspond to two types of City, and even less to some opposition between an ideal city (which is, in some sense, "celestial") and real cities (which are irremediably "earthly"). They represent two aspects of a single complex process or, if you prefer, two moments in a single dialectic. Every real city is always founded simultaneously on both an active genesis and a passive genesis: on a "free" (or rather, a liberating) rational agreement, on the one hand, and an imaginary agreement whose intrinsic ambivalence supposes the existence of a constraint, on the other. In the final analysis, there is no other cause of sociability than the striving of individuals to achieve self-preservation and, therefore, mutual utility. If, by some methodological fiction, we were to consider a certain number of "isolated" individuals, as Hobbes or Rousseau might have imagined them, we would have to see them as crushed by the power of their natural environment and unable in practice to protect themselves. Not only is the City inherently rational, but rational conduct always forms a part of the process by which it is constituted, whether the rationality behind it be economic, moral or intellectual. Without those affects which are related to reason (love and joy), no city would be able to survive. But no city can exist on a purely rational basis, since the mass of men, most of the time, are ruled by their passions, and not the reverse. Thus, if it is true that men do in fact live in cities or societies which are relatively stable, then it must be because, in some other way, the interplay of imagination and public constraint overdetermines and reinforces the collective logic of the individuals' interests. Above all, it is because the State obliges individuals to behave as if their lives were "guided by reason" and does so by working on their passions. In that case, should we say that, for Spinoza, the State is a necessary evil? Or is it rather a relative good (even if Spinoza insists on the fact that, in order to discipline the mob, which is "terrifying, if unafraid", the State and Religion must both resort to "sad" passions which are, in themselves, bad, such as Humility and Repentance [IVP54S])?

By going over this dialectic again, we have been able to explore further some of the consequences of Spinoza's definition of human nature. Reason and passion are both aspects of this nature, as they are of nature in general. Men are singular parts of nature, and we may tend to privilege them, but they bear no intrinsic title to special treatment. Reason is not above nature, and passion is not nature's "perversion". The construction of sociability and the City remains a process which is entirely immanent to nature, that is to say, which can be explained by determinate causes. Or better, it is precisely this dialectic of reason and passion, of utility and conflict, which enables us to grasp the form natural causality takes in the human order.

The Aporia of the Community and the Question of Knowledge

Nevertheless, the framework I have just outlined is still somewhat abstract. A genuine political theory cannot simply propose a series of principles of intelligibility. It must also try to account for the concrete realities of history, the singularity of existing political regimes, the immediate immanent causes of their stability and instability, and the conditions that enable men to increase their freedom and thus their own utility. It is in the two treatises (the *TTP* and the *TP*) that Spinoza addresses such concrete questions. As we have seen in the preceding chapters, there are considerable differences between the points of view of these two works. Doubtless, these differences could be explained by the circumstances in which they were written and by their author's strategic intention, both of which had changed in the intervening period. But since, from identical premises, these two works derive conclusions that partly contradict one another, this shift in perspective must also be analysed as a theoretical problem.

In the *TTP*, Spinoza presented the Republican regime of the United Provinces ("the Free Republic") as a democracy (or as the regime historically closest to a democracy) and defined democracy as "the most natural State". He represented the institution of democracy as the originating truth and model for every State, in the form of a contract (*pactum*) of association between individuals. By this contract, each individual transfers to the collective sovereign (of which he is himself one part) the right to legislate, to command and to punish crimes both public and private. The key word of this argument was freedom. On the one hand, "the purpose of the state is, in reality, freedom" (*TTP*, 293). On the other hand, the means by which the stability of the institutions can be guaranteed is freedom of opinion and of expression of opinion. Whenever these freedoms are abolished, the result is revolt and civil war. Conversely, whenever they exist, they enable the citizens to construct a common will and determine their common good. The crucial question which then arises is that of the relationship between religion and the City.

To resolve this question, Spinoza embarked upon an enormous digression, whose aim was nothing less than a total reform of the theological imagination. It is pointless to separate the private sphere from the public, to inscribe religious opinion in the private sphere and to establish a formal tolerance, if men continue to think that salvation on earth as in heaven depends upon subscribing to a given creed, and that the rejection of this creed by others is a threat to their own salvation. Such a belief is, in one sense, necessary, for no one can decide not to live his faith in accordance with his own temperament. And it can even be useful, since it encourages men to love their neighbours. Our aim, then, should be to change the content of faith itself, by extracting from Scripture a core of absolutely universal dogma. The content of this dogma would consist entirely of love for one's neighbour, hope for salvation and the affirmation of a divine Law that demands our obedience. It could then be shown that these dogmas are compatible with all philosophical opinions and with all individual variants of the representation of the divinity. It is therefore the responsibility of the (democratic) State to "demythicise" dogma by formulating this distinction and to impose it as a collective rule on all. It should not do this by itself taking the place of the Churches, but by controlling their public activities ("outward religion") and by establishing itself as the only authorised interpreter of the political consequences of faith (justice, charity and "works" in general), This solution clearly goes far beyond the classical idea of tolerance. On the one hand, it establishes a total equivalence and absolute equality of rights between all different confessions; on the other, it totally subordinates the apparatus of the Church to the apparatus of the State.

In formulating these theses, Spinoza was doubtless hoping to help combat the rising ride of fanaticism, which, in collusion with the monarchist party, threatened to take advantage of the masses' fear of looming war and crisis, and sweep the Republic away. Experience was – tragically – to show him both that his fears had not been vain and that the solution he had proposed was an illusion. It would seem that his reflections on the murder of the de Witt brothers led him to two conclusions. The first was that the Republican regime of the years 1650 to 1672 had not been a true "democracy", but rather an oligarchy whose inegalitarian forms had been one of the causes of social conflict. The second was that he had overestimated the effects of rational argument on the opinions of the masses (*vulgus, multitudo*) when it came to politics and theology. At a deeper level, he had overestimated their capacity to govern their own behaviour rationally and to rule themselves. It is true that these two propositions to some extent compensate for one another, for the intemperance of the masses is itself, in part, a consequence of the lack of democracy. But however that might be, he had certainly overestimated men's ability to establish, whatever the circumstances, and in conformity with "nature", a democratic regime.

In this context, we can read the completed chapters of the *TP* as the record of his conversion to a new way of seeing things. The question of freedom does not thereby disappear from view. On the contrary, Spinoza extends the scope of his inquiry into the conditions of freedom yet further. Now he wants to know how it can be guaranteed under different types of political regime, whatever the form that sovereignty takes (monarchy, aristocracy, democracy). But freedom is no longer the declared "purpose" of the state. The central preoccupation now is civil peace or *security* (*TP*, V, 2). The fundamental political question is therefore how to guarantee the stability of a political regime – to put it simply, how to prevent revolutions – by means of different systems of institutions. As a result, the idea of a social contract is no longer one of the foundations of the State. In its place there is the description of the process by which individuals with their natural right (that is, their own power) come to create a *collective individual*, that is, the State as an individual of individuals. This collective individual has a "body", which is produced by the combination of the bodily powers of each and every one, and a soul, which is the *idea* of that body. This soul has many functions: it is a way in which that body can be represented in imagination and in reason; it is the condition of effective decision (that is, government); and it is also an instrument for the expression of the collective passions.

Spinoza then recuperates a category that was at the centre of political debate at that time and gives it a bizarre twist. For him, the State is *absolute* when it is able to constitute itself as a stable individuality. His fundamental axiom, derived both from his own experience and from the "realist" political theorists (in particular, from Machiavelli), is that the greatest threat to the body politic is always internal conflict (in other words, its own citizens) and not external enemies. Thus, only a State which is organised to guarantee the security of its own citizens, and thus pre-empt and defuse conflicts that might be caused by differences of ideology or of class, can aspire to stability. In theory, every type of regime can achieve this and so can be "absolute". Democracy is no longer granted any theoretical superiority. Spinoza does assert that an effective democracy would be "the most absolute" State (*omnino absolutum*), that is, would combine the greatest possible freedom and equality with the greatest possible security. But he does not demonstrate his assertion, because the relevant chapters are missing. Besides, it would also seem that a democracy is the most difficult type of regime to establish.

It is understandable that many readers feel that in the *TP* Spinoza has reneged on his former ideas. A philosophy of freedom has been supplanted by a philosophy of the body social. The State founded on right has been replaced by a state founded on power. Yet it is precisely this distinction which, from Spinoza's point of view, is absurd. So this cannot be the correct interpretation. Let us go back then and look more closely at the internal logic of Spinoza's thought. Doubtless historical circumstance was decisive in inflecting the argument of the *TP* along new lines. But this in itself did not call into question the fundamental principle of his political theory and of his anthropology: the identity of right and power. It is this identity which founds Spinoza's project for the liberation of man. Why then does he now adopt a new model of the construction of the State? I believe that Spinoza came to realise that there was a contradiction in the model he had advanced in the *TTP*, which reflected an intrinsic weakness in his conception of "freedom". The *TP*, then, is remarkable as an attempt to overcome this weakness by incorporating into his theory what had been its original *other* – the nightmare that haunted it but also that it had failed, conceptually, to think through. This was the specific role of the masses (*multitudo*) and of mass movements in politics and history. Spinoza, then, has not lost sight of freedom to pursue security. He is simply trying to define the *real* conditions of freedom.

From this perspective, the *TTP* could be seen as one great negative argument, a *reductio ad absurdum*. If the rights–powers of individuals do not combine harmoniously, then civil society will be destroyed. We see this happening when the repression of opinions leads to ideological struggle and thus to the infernal cycle of revolution and counter-revolution. For individuals, the destruction of civil society is the immediate prelude to their own destruction. That is why men most often establish and respect rules by which their individual powers are combined. By encouraging the communication of opinions, these rules lead to a permanent transfer of power from individuals to the public authority. The practical result of this transfer (whether it takes the form of a tacit or a deliberate pact) is a multiplication of everyone's power, without distinction, that is, a multiplication of their right. In losing their absolute autonomy, State and individual have lost only a fictive freedom, a powerlessness. In return, they have actively committed themselves to the project of their own liberation.

The better the rule that governs the combination of powers is adapted to the diversity of individual desires and temperaments, the more effective its results will be. That is why the *TTP* specifies that the form of this rule should be total freedom of expression, limited only (but rigorously) by the need to guarantee obedience to the law (*TTP*, chapter XX). As we have seen, the essential meaning of such a rule is that *no one can be forced to think like another* or even to speak like another ("through another's mouth", as it were). Indeed, in the limiting case, this is a physical impossibility, since it would imply that the bodies in question are indistinguishable, in line with the political-religious fantasy of the "mystical body". If these conditions are observed, then the State can be supposed to be the collective author of every individual action that is in conformity with the law, because the actual cause of the actions of the State (first among them, the establishment of the law) is the reciprocal action of individuals who find in the State's existence the means to their utility or their pleasure.

"If under civil law *only deeds were arraigned, and words were not punished*", then that sedition which is due to the fact that the "law intrudes into the realm of speculative thought, and beliefs are put on trial and condemned as crimes" would be rendered impossible (*TTP*, 51), and its illegitimacy would be immediately obvious. Thus monarchy and aristocracy tend to destroy themselves, whereas a democratic regime is able to know its own limits and can thus work to extend them indefinitely.

This argument is very fine and very plausible. It embodies a good many of the motivations that lead philosophers and citizens throughout history to see themselves as democrats. However, it turns out to be untenable. To begin with, it contains an internal contradiction that is visible both in practice and by comparison with the anthropology of the *Ethics*. The whole of the *TTP*'s "democratic" solution rests on the possibility of making a clear distinction between *speech* and *thought*, on the one hand, and *actions*, on the other. But the idea of a "right" is then no longer equivalent to power. It has reverted to being a formal criterion, which is asserted a priori by some authority. From the perspective of power, which is that of reality, the words and thoughts which are most effective – and in particular those which attack injustice and the evils of the present State – are themselves actions. They are, in fact, the most dangerous actions of all, for they inevitably incite other men to think and act in their turn. Thus, this criterion turns out to be unusable precisely where it is most indispensable. Spinoza himself discovered the truth of this when he came to publish the *TTP*. Of course, we might say that the issue here is in fact that of constituting a *consensus* on the need for a social pact and for fundamental democratic values. But such a consensus only exists when the State is not corrupt or, as Spinoza would say, "violent". If we follow this line of argument then, we are led into an infinite regression. This regression is, in one sense, what is most interesting about the *TTP*. In order to guarantee that the civil pact will hold, it is necessary to double it up with a religious pact, that is, with an agreement on those demands of faith which are common to all theological tendencies. A religious pact in turn supposes some common bond of passion. Spinoza identifies this bond as patriotism. But the notion of a *democratic patriotism* would inevitably be torn between nationalism (the ideology of the divine election of a people) and universalism (the assertion of the identity of citizen and neighbour). This is more than simply problematical. In fact, we have found our way back into the same vicious circle from which we began.

It is this aporia, then, which Spinoza sets out to study in the *TP*. How can one produce a *consensus*, not just in the sense of the communication of pre-existing opinions, but above all as the condition of the creation of *communicable opinions* (that is, opinions which are not mutually exclusive)? And how can this consensus be produced since, as we have seen, the "matter" of politics is constituted not of isolated individuals but of a *mass*, whose most frequent passion is fear, and to which everyone belongs, rulers and ruled alike? For a mass, in this sense, is a fearful thing, not only to those who govern, but even to itself (*terrere, nisi paveant*).

This perspective was imposed on Spinoza both by the historical circumstances and by the internal difficulties of his own theory. It led him to examine in detail the modes of operation of the *institutions*. These institutions are not only *laws* (*leges*) but also the "apparatus of the State" (*imperium*), which is composed of an administration and systems of policing, representation, decision and control. They thus imply a distribution of powers, of public offices and of social conditions, which will differ from one regime to another (monarchy, unitary or federal aristocracy, democracy). That is, the institutions organise the relation between the rulers and the ruled, considered as classes. Spinoza does not give up on his idea that individuals are always in the final analysis motivated by the desire for their own preservation and thus by the search for what is most useful to them. But he totally abandons the idea that the State is constructed on the basis of "independent" powers. To put it another way, he banishes every remaining trace of the fiction of a state of nature that was left in the idea of a social *pact* agreed between individuals who were simply juxtaposed with one another. For individuals are *not* independent (*sui juris*), they can only become so, to a greater or lesser degree. Thus, the essential importance of the institutions as a problem for political theory derives from the fact that *the true matter of politics is the mass*. When individuals represent their interests to themselves, that is, when they think and act, they do so in imaginary forms that are always already collective forms (stories that bear the hopes and fears of a group).

The institution of the "body politic" can then be understood as a process of *internal* transformation of the power of the mass (*potentia multitudinis*), through which that power which was passive tends to become active. This activity is both a self-limitation and a self-organisation. The passive mass is ignorant of itself, so it inevitably fluctuates under the influence of fortune between over-estimation and under-estimation of its own power. This leads it to alternate between submission and revolt, between devotion to its "prophets" and the "great men" sent by Providence, and hatred of those who govern it. The active mass, on the other hand, is simply a collectivity of citizens, who are enabled by their institutions to reach decisions, to supervise their application and to correct their effects. These decisions will take different forms according to the historical circumstances, the nature of property rights, the level of the general culture and national traditions.

When the mass is fully active (that is, perfectly instituted), then the State has achieved what for Spinoza is the *absolute* of power – internal stability, which approximates in human terms "a kind of eternity".[7] But this concept clearly corresponds to a "striving" (a tendency) rather than to a static state. That is why, paradoxically, the fact that the *TP* remained unfinished has a theoretical advantage: instead of a *theory of democracy* what we have is a theory of *democratisation*, which is valid for *every* regime. The modalities employed may vary, but there is one fundamental mechanism which is always the same and to which Spinoza continually returns. This is the circulation of information, which will tend both to guarantee that the actions of the government and the motives for its decisions receive the greatest possible publicity (thus opposing the tradition of the *arcana imperii* or *secret d'Etat*)[8] and to educate the citizens themselves by exercising their judgement on public affairs. Spinoza shows that secrecy surrounding power is not an effect of the incompetence and violence of those who are governed, but their cause (*TP*, VII, 27).

The result is that the "absolute" State is also a State in which the ruling class is continuously expanding. Spinoza develops this hypothesis with special reference to the aristocratic regime, to the point of claiming that the ruling class must constitute a majority of the citizens![9] This hypothesis has a corollary: the institutions must bring about the conditions for the greatest possible diversification of opinion, so that the decisions they produce can effectively be based on the combination of all existing points of view. This explains Spinoza's hostility to political-religious parties, not because

[7] The celebrated formula *species aeternitatis* or *sub aeternitatis specie* is central to the definition of the "third kind of knowledge" (that of "singular things") in the *Ethics*, VP22ff. The idea of eternity reappears in the *TP*, VIII, 3 and X, 1–2 in a different context, where Spinoza deals with the conditions that can guarantee the stability of a regime for an indefinite period of time. The basic issue remains, however, that of the power of an "individual".

[8] On the idea of the *"secret d'Etat"* and its function in pre-classical theories of power, cf. Michel Senellart, *Machiavélisme et raison d'Etat. XIIe–XVIIIe siècle* (Paris: Presses Universitaires de France, 1989); *Les arts de gouverner. Du regimen médiéval au concept de gouvernement* (Paris: Seuil, 1995).

[9] It would be interesting to compare at length Locke's concept of the republic as a state founded on the rule of the majority and Spinoza's concept of democracy as a limiting concept, or goal, for the transformation of the ruling class into a majority.

they are at odds with public opinion but because they are mechanisms for reducing its complexity, by channelling it into pre-established categories. They thus distort the attempt to reach general decisions that will serve the interests of the people as a whole. The more adequately the mass comes to know itself, that is, comes to know the different singularities from which it is composed, the less likely it will be to take fright at itself. And vice versa.

Let me conclude by going back schematically over five points that have arisen from this argument.

First, Spinoza's politics confirms, in concrete terms, everything his metaphysics would have led us to expect. The dualisms that had structured anthropology, morality and politics since antiquity are radically displaced. These include the dualism of nature and culture (institutions, artifice), which is responsible for the question of whether the individual or society should be considered "natural"; the dualism of soul and body (of the spiritual and the material), which is the origin of our hierarchical vision of the individual and society; and, above all, the moral dualism of goodness and perversity, which is the source of the opposition between those philosophers for whom "no one is voluntarily wicked" (Plato) or for whom man is naturally good to his fellow man (Rousseau), and those such as Machiavelli and Hobbes, who base their conception of social relations on the hypothesis of human wickedness, or at least on the idea that the hold their interests have over them leads men to behave *as if* they hated one another. In the place of these essentialist alternatives, Spinoza establishes an analytic of desire and of its multiple forms, ranged around the polarity of activity and passivity.

Second, for Spinoza, nature is also history: a history without purpose, indeed, but not without a process, not without a movement of transformation (that is to say, no particular transformation is ever "guaranteed"). By analysing all the possible historical configurations of the "dialectic" between reason and passion that structures the life of the City, we come to know human nature itself – and thus, nature in general. But politics is the touchstone of historical knowledge. So if we know politics rationally – as rationally as we know mathematics – then we know God, for God conceived adequately is identical with the multiplicity of natural powers.

Third, freedom does not need to be added to nature or promised as another "kingdom" that is to come. Freedom is certainly opposed to constraint – the stronger the constraint, the less freedom one has – but it is not opposed to determinism or, rather, to determination, that is, it does not consist in the absence of causes for human action. It is neither a right that we acquire at birth nor an eschatological perspective that is indefinitely deferred. For our *liberation has always already begun*. It is the *conatus* itself, the movement by which activity preponderates over passivity. But this has the corollary that liberation is always still a "striving" to exist adequately, through the knowledge of our causes. In practice, if imagination is the field of politics – the "matter" of social relationships – and if the hopes and fears of the masses – love and hate for our "fellow men" – are inherent in the collective imagination, then the State is the necessary instrument of our liberation. But this is so only on condition that it too is striving to liberate itself. Only the State which is permanently working to advance its own process of democratisation can "organise the State [*imperium*] so that all its members, rulers as well as ruled, do what the common welfare requires whether they wish it or not" (*TP*, VI, 3), becoming thus ever more useful to each other.

Fourth, the difference between those who rule and those who are ruled is a difference between a dominating and a dominated class for many different reasons. But this difference finally comes to focus on a monopoly of knowledge at the level of the State, in whose name obedience is demanded. This intrinsically ambivalent situation can easily be reversed, for the insecurity of the State is bound up with individuals' ignorance of who they themselves are, and of how they are affected by their mutual dependency. The history of theocratic states shows how the monopoly of knowledge turns into a monopoly of ignorance (and we could say the same of the technocratic states in which we live today). On the other hand, those "living" institutions which can bring about the democratisation of the State are also those which make knowledge available, and thus are the condition by which knowledge is actually constituted as such. They are therefore not simply an external condition of knowledge or wisdom, but an intrinsic condition. The autarky of the wise man and that of the philosopher-king are, in this perspective, both equally absurd.

Fifth, the problem of political communication, as discussed by Spinoza, allows us to go beyond the alternative between individualism and organicism (or corporatism) as it has been understood by political philosophy from antiquity to the present day – that is, as a question of *origin*, of *foundation*. Nevertheless, for Spinoza the issue is still whether what is given at the outset is the individual (conceived of as an archetype or as a random example of humanity, a "man without qualities") or the "sociable animal" of Aristotle and the scholastics, the "Great Being" of Auguste Comte (for whom the individual is a mere abstraction). As we have seen, for Spinoza the concept of the individual is absolutely central, but it has "several meanings". The individual is neither created by God according to an eternal model nor delivered by nature as a kind of raw material. The individual is a construction. This construction is the result of a striving (*conatus*) by the individual himself, within the determinate conditions of his "way of life". And that "way of life" is nothing other than a given *regime of communication* (affective, economic or intellectual) with other individuals. The different regimes of communication form a sequence through which a collective effort is being worked out – the effort to transform the mode of communication, to move from relationships of identification (that is, from the mode of *communion*) to relationships based on *exchange* of goods and of knowledge. The political state itself is essentially one such regime. But Spinoza's definition of the State, although still rigorously realistic, is clearly also much *broader* than the juridical and administrative form that is referred to by that name in the modern period (that is, the period of the bourgeois nation-state). Thus, this definition can help us to envisage, at least in theory, historical forms of the State other than the present form. And it also identifies for us the decisive mechanism by which those new forms can be created: the democratisation of knowledge.

CHRONOLOGY

1536	Calvin publishes the *Institutes of the Christian Religion*.
1565	Revolt of the Gueuzen.
1568	Outbreak of the war of independence in the Spanish Netherlands (the Eighty Years' War).
1579	The "Union of Utrecht": foundation of the United Provinces.
1594	Publication in Poland of Socinus's treatise on the doctrine of the atonement, *De Christo Servatore*.
c.1600	**Emigration of the Espinosa family from Portugal to Nantes, then to Amsterdam.**
1602	Foundation of the Dutch East India Company.
1603	Arminius is appointed to the faculty of theology in Leiden, where Gomar also teaches; their disputes about tolerance and free will intensify.
1609	The Twelve Years' Truce; foundation of the Bank of Amsterdam.
1610	Uytenbogaert, disciple of Arminius and adviser to Oldenbarnevelt, writes the Remonstrants' manifesto.
1614	Hugh de Groot begins work on his *De Imperio Summarum Potestarum Circa Sacra* (published posthumously in 1647).
1619	Synod of Dort, condemning Arminianism; execution of Oldenbarnevelt; foundation of the Collegiants. The Thirty Years' War begins (Descartes joins Maurice of Nassau's army as a volunteer).
1621	War resumes in Holland.
1628	Descartes moves to Holland.
1632	**Birth of Baruch d'Espinosa in Amsterdam.**

1633   Trial and definitive condemnation of Galileo in Rome. At the last minute, Descartes decides not to publish his treatise, *The World*.

1638   Galileo's *Dialogue Concerning Two New Sciences* is smuggled to Holland and published in Leiden by Louis Elzevirs. Foundation of the great "Portuguese" synagogue in Amsterdam; **Spinoza studies at the rabbinic school.**

1639   Naudé, the "libertine" theorist, publishes his *Political Considerations on Coups d'Etat*, inspired by Machiavelli.

1639–40 The Bishops' War in Scotland.

1640   Jansenius's *Augustinus* is published posthumously.

1641   Descartes publishes his *Meditations on First Philosophy*.

1642   Outbreak of the English Civil War; Hobbes publishes his *De Cive*.

1644   Milton publishes the *Areopagitica*, his manifesto for the freedom of the press.

1645   Herbert of Cherbury publishes his *De Religione Laici* and *De Causis Errorum*; they will be followed in 1663 by the *De Religione Gentilium*.

1648   Peace of Münster: the United Provinces are definitively independent; in France, the beginning of the Fronde (which will last until 1653).

1649   Execution of Charles I of England.

1650   William II of Orange's unsuccessful coup d'Etat; William II dies in November; his son, the future William III, is born a week later; Johan de Witt is made Councillor Pensionary of Holland.

1651   Cromwell institutes the Navigation Act; Hobbes publishes his *Leviathan*.

1654   The post of stadholder is abolished in Holland.

1656   **Spinoza is banished from the Jewish community of Amsterdam. He studies the Latin humanities, science and philosophy at the school of the former Jesuit, Van den Enden.**

1660   Restoration of the Stuarts in England. **Spinoza is obliged to leave Amsterdam: he goes to live with the Collegiants of Rijnsburg and works on a *Treatise on the Emendation of the Intellect*, which he never completed (published in 1677).**

1661   Beginning of the "personal reign" of Louis XIV.

1662   Charter of incorporation of the Royal Society, of which Oldenburg is the secretary; among the members are Boyle and Newton.

1663   **Spinoza moves to Voorburg; he publishes *Descartes' Principles of Philosophy*, followed by an appendix, his *Metaphysical Thoughts*.**

1665   Beginning of the second Anglo-Dutch War.

1668   Condemnation of Adriaan Koerbagh, a disciple of Spinoza.

1670   **Spinoza publishes the *Tractatus Theologico-Politicus* anonymously;** in France, the *Pensées* of Pascal are published posthumously.

1671   **Spinoza moves to The Hague; he has the Dutch translation of the *TTP* stopped, probably at the request of Johan de Witt.**

1672   Louis XIV invades Holland; the de Witt brothers are killed by the mob; William III becomes stadholder.

1673   **Spinoza turns down a chair of philosophy at Heidelberg; he is invited to visit the Prince de Condé's camp.** Huygens publishes his *Horologium Oscillatorium* (on the theory of the pendulum and the construction of chronometers).

1674   The Estates-General of Holland condemns the *TTP* along with other "heretical" or "atheistic" writings. Malebranche publishes volume I of his *Search After Truth*, which was to be accused of containing "Spinozist" theses.

1675   **Spinoza completes the *Ethics* but decides not to publish it, and begins writing the *Tractatus Politicus*.**

1676   **Leibniz visits Spinoza.** The synod of The Hague orders a "search" for the author of the *TTP*.

1677   **Death of Spinoza.** His friends publish the *Opera Posthuma*, which will be condemned the following year.

1681   Bossuet writes the *Politics Derived from Holy Scripture*, publishes his *Discourse on Universal History* and has Richard Simon's *Critical History of the Old Testament* (whose method resembles that of the *TTP*) banned.

1685   Revocation of the Edict of Nantes.
1687   Newton (influenced by "Unitarian" theology) publishes
         the *Principia Mathematica*.
1688   The Glorious Revolution: William III becomes King of
         England.
1689   Locke publishes *A Letter Concerning Tolerance*, followed
         in 1690 by his *Two Treatises of Government*.
1697   In his *Historical and Critical Dictionary*, Bayle defines
         Spinoza as a "systematic atheist" who was strangely
         virtuous.
1710   Leibniz publishes his *Theodicy*, an indirect reply to
         Spinoza.

FURTHER READING

The Life

There is no English-language equivalent of the excellent German biography by Theun de Vries, *Spinoza in Selbstzeugnissen und Bilddokumenten* (Hamburg: Rowohlt Taschenbuch, 1970).

The Historical Context

Fernand Braudel, *Civilization and Capitalism, 15th–18th Century: Perspective of the World*, vol. 3 (London: Fontana, 1985), esp. chapter 3.

Leszek Kolakowski, *Swiadomosc religijina i wizz koscielna* (Warsaw, 1965). This seminal work is still not available in English; a French edition exists, under the title *Chrétiens sans église* (Paris: Gallimard, 1969).

Robert Mandrou, *L'Europe "absolutiste", raison et raison d'état, 1649–1775* (Paris: Fayard, 1977).

Friedrich Meinecke, *The Doctrine of Raison d'État and its Place in Modern History*, Douglas Scott, trans. (London: Routledge and Kegan Paul, 1957).

K. O. Meinsma, *Spinoza en zijn kring* (The Hague, 1896). There is no English translation of this great work. A French translation, revised and updated by a team of French and Dutch scholars, is available under the title *Spinoza et son cercle* (Paris: Vrin, 1983).

Douglas Nobbs, *Theocracy and Toleration* (Cambridge: Cambridge University Press, 1938).

Herbert H. Rowen, *John de Witt, Grand Pensionary of Holland, 1625–1672* (Princeton, N.J.: Princeton University Press, 1978).

Paul Vernière, *Spinoza et la pensée française avant la Révolution*, 2nd ed. (Paris: Presses Universitaires de France, 1982).

Immanuel Wallerstein, *Modern World System: Mercantilism and the Consolidation of the European World Economy, 1600–1750*, vol. 2 (London and NY: Academic Press, 1980), esp. chapter 2.

Spinoza and Politics

Of the books that have been particularly influential on my own thinking, three are currently available in English translation:

Gilles Deleuze, *Expressionism in Philosophy: Spinoza*, Martin Joughin, trans. (Zone Books, 1990).

Gilles Deleuze, *Spinoza, practical philosophy*, R. Hurley, trans. (San Francisco: City Lights Books, 1988).

Antonio Negri, *Savage Anomaly: Power of Spinoza's Metaphysics and Politics*, M. Hardt, trans. (Minneapolis: University of Minnesota Press, 1991).

Much of the recent French scholarship which has helped me in elaborating my own ideas is, however, unavailable in English. I list here some of the more important works.

Michèle Bertrand, *Spinoza et l'imaginaire* (Paris: Presses Universitaires de France, 1983).

Stanislas Breton, *Spinoza, théologie et politique* (Paris: Desclée, 1977).

Alexandre Matheron, *Individu et communauté chez Spinoza* (Paris: Minuit, 1969); *Le Christ et le salut des ignorants chez Spinoza* (Paris: Aubier-Montaigne, 1971); *Anthropologie et politique au XVIIe siècle (Etudes sur Spinoza)* (Paris: Vrin, 1986).

André Tosel, *Spinoza ou le crépuscule de la servitude* (Paris: Aubier-Montaigne, 1984).

Sylvain Zac, *Spinoza et l'interprétation de l'écriture* (Paris: Presses Universitaires de France, 1965); *Philosophie, théologie, politique dans l'oeuvre de Spinoza* (Paris: Vrin, 1979).

Also invaluable are:

Spinoza nell' 350 Anniversario della nascita, Proceedings of the First Italian International Congress on Spinoza, Emilia Giancotti, ed. (Napoli: Bibliopolis, 1985).

Studia Spinozana, vol. 1 (Alling: Walther & Walther, 1985).

Other relevant works in English

Edwin Curley, *Behind the Geometrical Method: A Reading of Spinoza's Ethics* (Princeton, N.J.: Princeton University Press, 1988).

Douglas J. Den Uyl, *Power, State and Freedom. An Interpretation of Spinoza's Political Philosophy* (Assen: Van Gorcum, 1983).

C. De Deugd, ed., *Spinoza's Political and Theological Thought* (Amsterdam and New York: North Holland Publishing Company, 1984).

Richard H. Popkin, *The History of Scepticism from Erasmus to Spinoza*, rev. and exp. edn. (Berkeley and Los Angeles: University of California Press, 1979).

Leo Strauss, *Spinoza's Critique of Religion*, E. M. Sinclair, trans. (New York: Schocken Books, 1965).

INDEX

Althusser, Louis viii–ix, xi, xii
Anabaptists 21
Anderson, Perry xi
  Considerations on Western Marxism viii,
    ix
aristocracy 56, 68, 71–3
Aristotle 124
  Politics 52
Armenianism
  condemned by Synod of Dort 21–2
  free will 11, 20
  split in Dutch Calvinism 18–19
St Augustine of Hippo 10

Balibar, Etienne
  Reading Capital viii
  "Spinoza, the Anti-Orwell" x
Bayle, Pierre xxi, 1, 100
body *see* soul and body
Bossuet, Jacques Bénigne 77

Calvinists xv
  accuse Spinoza of atheism 6
  censorship of Spinoza 52–3
  Gomarists 19–20
  image of God 14
  Orange-Nassau princes protect 22
  question of grace 10, 18–19
  reform within Dutch Republic 18
Catholicism 11
Christianity
  anti-Trinitarian sects 21
  grace and salvation 10–11
  historical progress 39–42
  image of God 15
  society 78
citizenship 34
class 111
Collegiants 21
Colletti, Lucio viii

communication 124
  and ethics 95–8
  and knowledge 101
  modes of 101
  producing consensus 119–20
  reason 95–7
Comte, Auguste 124
Considerations on Western Marxism
    (Anderson) viii, ix
Cromwell, Oliver 39

De Cive (Hobbes) 54
decision
  aristocracy 71–3
  individuals 71
  majority rule 73–4
  monarchy 71–3, 75
Deleuze, Gilles
  Spinoza et le problème de l'expression xii
democracy
  bourgeois monarchy 74–5
  governability of the masses 58
  individuals participate in state 30–31
  the king as the mind of the multitude
    72–3
  loss by intemperance of masses 115–16
  majority rule 73–4
  the most natural state 31–6, 114
  self-restraint and balance 69–71
  social covenant 119–22
  Spinoza's new view 116–17
  within theocracy 47–8
  unfinished argument in the *TP* 56–8
Descartes, René
  Metaphysical Meditations 6
desire 122
  defining 107–8
  for the good of others 110
  for knowledge 107
  soul and body 105–6

Dieu: Ethique I (Gueroult) xii
Dutch Republic
  Calvinist reform 18–22
  commercial expansion xiv, xv
  monarchists 3
  Orange dynasty 16–18, 52
  Spinoza's worries 3–5, 114–15
  threat to republicanism xv–xviii
duty 60

Engels, Friedrich ix
Erasmus, Desiderius 18
Ethics (Spinoza)
  communication 95–8
  desire is man's essence 105–13
  Marxists ix
  men desire good for self and other
    men 78–88
  Neo-Platonism xiv
  obedience 88–95
  theory of imagination 9
  withheld for political reasons 53
  writing and publication 76

faith 6, 9
free will and predestination
  Armenianism 18
  debate about grace 10–11
  within natural laws 12–14
  question of grace and salvation 10–11
  rights of individuals 60
freedom 3–5, 123
  natural right 55–6, 100–101
  obedience 91–5
  passion and reason 63
  from right 104
  of thought 25–31, 50, 114

God
  anthropomorphic imagination 14–16
  continuous production 65
  freedom of power 59
  independence 61
  man's fear of 47
  Marxism ix
  and nature 99–100
  necessity brings obedience 92
  political representatives on earth 48
  virtue of social relations 78, 79
  will maintained in Nature 12–14
Gomarists 19–20, 22
good and evil 88
Greece
  society 77, 78
Groot, Hugh de (Grotius)
  Of the Power of the Sovereign 19

Gueroult, Martial
  Dieu: Ethique I xii

Harmensen, Jacob (Arminius) 11
Hebrew state 41–2
  historical narrative 37–9
  theocracy 45
Hegel, Georg W. F. xiii–xiv
Hegel ou Spinoza (Macherey) xiii–xiv
history xv
  Christianity 39–42
  the Hebrew state 37–9
  human nature 122–3
  narrative 37–8
  naturalism 36–7, 44
  progress 39
Hobbes, Thomas
  De Cive 54
  governing the multitude 69
  individual freedom 55–6
  Leviathan 54–6, 64
  right and power 104
  warring society 77
Huygens, Christiaan 19

identification 111
imagination
  anthropomorphic picture of God
    14–16
  general theory of 9
  ingenium 29
  interaction with reason 109–10
Individu et communauté chez Spinoza
    (Matheron) xii
individuals xvii–xviii
  active and passive 94–5, 122
  and Christ's teachings 40
  communication 124
  contractual relations 62
  decision 71
  defining man in body and soul 105–6
  desire for virtue 79–80
  freedom of thought 25–31
  give power to public 112–13
  human perfection 100
  independence and dependence 61, 63
  participation in state 30–31
  respect for rules 117–18
  right to freedom 55–6, 104
  right to power 4, 59–60
  single beings within nature 84
  singular and general 107–8
  state as individual of individuals 64–7
  violence against state 68
ingenium 29
  democracy 49

ingenium (*cont*.)
  nations 37
  political order 66
  social relations 79
Israel, Menasseh ben 21

Jansenists 11
Jesuits 11
Jews *see also* Hebrew state
  community in Amsterdam 18, 22–3

Kant, Immanuel
  universal law 110
knowledge 123–4 *see also* reason
  and affectivity 108–9
  communication 101
  democratisation 124
  individual reason 96–7
  intuitive 97–8
  as political praxis 98
  superstition 97, 98
  true idea of singular things 102
Koerbagh, Adriaan 23
Kolakowski, Leszek 20

language 97
L'anomalia selvaggia (Negri) xiv
laws
  covenant versus divine law 49
  Mosaic 45, 47
  natural 12–14
  religion 43
  theocracy 47
Leviathan (Hobbes) 54, 64
liberalism x–xi
love
  basis of true religion 11
  for neighbours 11, 48–9, 111–12, 123

Macherey, Pierre xi
  Hegel ou Spinoza xiii–xiv
Machiavelli, Niccolo 53–4
Marx, Karl
  prehistory of dialectical materialism
    viii–ix
  social relations 77
masses xvii *see also* democracy
  intemperance loses democracy 115–16
  king as the mind of 72–3
  violence 105
materialism xi
  Tractatus-Theologico Politicus xiv
Matheron, Alexandre 38
  Individu et communauté chez Spinoza xii
Maurice of Nassau 17
Mennonites 21

Metaphysical Meditations (Descartes) 6
Meyer, Louis 53
monarchy
  bourgeois monarch 75
  decision 71–3
  divine right 55–6
  and religion 43–4
  sedition 68
  Spinoza's unfinished argument in the
    TP 56–8
morality
  social relations 78–80
Moses 37, 41
  prophetic theology 9–10

naturalism 36–7, 44
nature 99–100
  natural laws and will of God 12–14
Negri, Antonio
  L'anomalia selvaggia xiv
neighbours
  contrary passions of love and hate
    111–12
  love for 11, 48–9, 123
  obedience to law as loyalty 93
  suspicion of 47
Neo-Platonism xiv
The Netherlands *see* Dutch Republic
nominalism 107–8

obedience 88–95, 91, 92, 123
Of the Power of the Sovereign (de Groot) 19
Oldenbarnevelt, Jan van 17
Orange-Nassau dynasty xv, 16–18, 22
original sin 11

passion *see also* desire
  affective genius 110–11
  ambition 111
  conflicting 111–12
  and knowledge 108–9
  obedience 94
  and reason 63
  social relations 85–8
St Paul 10, 40
philosophy 6–9
Platonism 53–4
politics *see also* state
  Machiavelli defended 53–4
  purpose 64
Politics (Aristotle) 52
power *see also* state
  absolute 121
  arbitrary use 67
  equivalence of right and de facto
    power 63

power (*cont.*)
  individual gives to public 112
  individuals' rights 4, 59–63, 117–18
  reciprocal action 66–7
  religious leaders 48
  right 103–5
  risk in severe enforcement 62
Protestantism 10–11

Quakers 22

reason
  communication 95–7
  Descartes 6
  interaction with imagination 109–10
  obedience 93–4
religion
  force of law 43
  formulating arguments xv–xvi
  inner and outward 18–19, 30, 44, 115
  laws 45
  Mosaic 9–10
  neighbourly love 11
  in opposition to state 29
  revealed/true 6–9
  Spinoza worries about fanaticism 115
  theocracy 44–8
  TTP's reception 1–2
right
  equality 62
  equivalence of right and de facto
    power 63
  and freedom 100–101
  of individuals 59–63, 104, 117–18
  natural 104–5
  of passion 63
  as power 103–5
Rousseau, Jean-Jacques 77

salvation
  Mosaic theology 10
  within the natural world 13–14
  obedience 93
  perceived threat of other creeds
    114–15
  question of grace 10–11
sedition 118
social covenant xiv, 27, 33, 55, 93
  trying to hold consensus 119–22
social relations
  body-soul parallel 106–7
  communication 95–8
  desire for common good 78–88,
    110–11
  historical approaches to society 76–8
  identification 111

obedience 88–95
passion 85–8
reason 83–4
Socinians 21, 53
soul and body 89–91, 90, 100
  desire 105–6
  metaphorical relation to individuals and
    state 106–7
Spinoza, Baruch de *see also Ethics*;
    Tractatus Politicus; *Tractatus Theologico-
    Politicus*
  changes in last years 50–51
  effect of political events 52–4
  family and background 22–3
  and Hegel xiii–xiv
  individual in society xvii–xviii
  motivations to write *TTP* 5–6
  prehistory of dialectical materialism viii
  Treatise on the Emendation of the Intellect
    96, 101–2
  works split by followers 102–3
  worries about fanaticism 115
"Spinoza, the Anti-Orwell" (Balibar) x
Spinoza et le problème de l'expression
    (Deleuze) xii
state *see also* democracy; monarchy
  administration 74
  and church 18–19
  conflicting passions 112–14
  continuous production 65
  decision 71–5
  democracy as natural 31–6
  fear and revolution 35–6, 38–9, 68
  freedom of thought 25–31
  Gomarist movement 20
  as individual of individuals 64–7, 116
  individuals' participation 30–31
  institutions 120
  internal conflict greatest threat 116
  juridical absolutism 55
  metaphorical relation to soul and body
    106–7
  obedience 88–95, 123
  reciprocal action 66–9
  religions struggling against 29
  right as power 103–5
  security 51, 56, 66
  sedition 118
  self-limitation 31, 69–71
  separation from church 27
  social covenant 119–22
  theocracy 44–8
  theoretical and practical attributes of
    sovereignty 34–5
  TTP's reception 2
superstition 9

superstition (*cont.*)
    and knowledge 97, 98, 109
Synod of Dort 21

Thalheimer, August viii
theocracy 44–8, 51
    democracy within 47–8
    political representatives of God 48
thought
    versus actions 119
    freedom of 25–31, 50, 114, 118
Tosel, André ix
Tractatus Politicus (Spinoza)
    compared to *TTP* 50–52
    freedom and obedience 93
    plan of unfinished argument 56–8
    right as power 103
    Spinoza's new view of democracy
        116–22
    Spinoza's political milieu 52–4
Tractatus Theologico-Politicus (Spinoza) ix

civil pact 118–19
compared to *TP* 51
context of Dutch Republic xvi–xviii,
    22–4
freedom of thought within state 25–31
materialism xiv
negative reaction to publication 1–5
right as power 103
separation of theology and philosophy
    6–9
social contract xiv
Treatise on the Emendation of the Intellect
    (Spinoza) 96, 101–2
truth 4, 9

Unitarians 21

Velthuysen, Lambert de 55

William of Orange 17
Witt, Johan de 17, 19, 23, 115